SELECTED
POEMS

Robert Gray

SELECTED
POEMS

ANGUS
& ROBERTSON
PUBLISHERS

To Dee Jones

Arts for
Australians
Australia Council

*Collins/Angus & Robertson Publishers'
creative writing programme is
assisted by the Australia Council,
the Australian government's arts advisory
and support organisation.*

ANGUS & ROBERTSON PUBLISHERS

*Unit 4, Eden Park, 31 Waterloo Road,
North Ryde, NSW, Australia 2113;
94 Newton Road, Auckland 1,
New Zealand; and
16 Golden Square, London W1R 4BN,
United Kingdom*

*First published in Australia
by Angus & Robertson Publishers in 1985
This revised and expanded edition
published in 1990*

*National Library of Australia
Cataloguing-in-publication data.*

Gray, Robert, 1945–
  Selected poems.

  ISBN 0 207 16647 1.

  I. Title. (Series: A & R modern poets).

A821.3

*Typeset in 10/12 pt Andover by Midland Typesetters
Printed in Australia by Griffin Press*

AUTHOR'S NOTE

Although called a *Selected Poems*, this book, in the present revised edition, contains all my work that I find worth preserving, in the form I consider resolved. Other poems, from books, an early pamphlet, and magazines, received my attention, but resisted it, and I trust will now be left in oblivion, along with earlier versions of the poems that are here.

One poem from *Creekwater Journal*, "On Climbing the Stone Gate Peak", has been taken for a translation, or "version", but although it is ascribed to an historical figure—a poet, who invented mountaineering boots—it is original. The second section of "At the Inlet", in *The Skylight*, is a quotation from Karl Jaspers (whose ideas I don't otherwise share).

In collecting these poems, I would again like to acknowledge the Literature Board of the Australia Council for the fellowships which have helped with the writing of most of them.

CONTENTS

CREEKWATER
JOURNAL

Journey: The North Coast

Next thing, I wake up in a swaying bunk,
as though on board a clipper
lying in the sea,
and it's the train, that booms and cracks,
it tears the wind apart.
Now the man's gone
who had the bunk below me. I swing out,
cover his bed and rattle up the sash—
there's sunlight rotating
off the drab carpet. And the water sways
solidly in its silver basin, so cold
it joins together through my hand.
I see from where I'm bent
one of those bright crockery days
that belong to so much I remember.
The train's shadow, like a bird's,
flees on the blue and silver paddocks,
over fences that look split from stone,
and banks of fern,
a red clay bank, full of roots,
over a dark creek, with logs and leaves suspended,
and blackened tree trunks.
Down these slopes move, as a nude descends a staircase,
slender white gum trees,
and now the country bursts open on the sea—
across a calico beach, unfurling;
strewn with flakes of light
that make the whole compartment whirl.
Shuttering shadows. I rise into the mirror
rested. I'll leave my hair
ruffled a bit that way—fold the pyjamas,
stow the book and wash bag. Everything done,
press down the latches into the case,
that for twelve months I've watched standing out
of a morning, above the wardrobe
in a furnished room.

A Kangaroo

That hungry face
moves on grass
the way an artist's pencil
retouches
shadows.

Then, when he's bounding,
the head's borne
refined as a deer's, relaxed,
before
a powerful tight basketball attack.

And the toe-nail, in the forefront,
a stevedore's claw
(tears with it, cantilevered on his tail);
the forepaws
are a housedog's, begging.

So that here,
sitting up and simply, is the unknown
energy, which is nature,
that's able to spawn, as one,
every extreme thing.

The Hospital

All day, I've escaped within this book.
Now dusk comes
soaking slowly into the compartments
of a high, bare window.
And I lie down inside these immaculate strong sheets,

3

where I am going to be
a long
time. From one of the other dimly-
lighted beds, that are drifting with me
through these days, the faint
sounds of a radio. And a nurse
flickers by
out in the corridor; that squeaking
vinyl. There are tea trays,
somewhere near. Beyond the window's cruciform
comes Venus,
a star like thistledown.
Church bells have begun ringing, far off,
on the dark clouds,
and I hear the sounds of children, running about late,
down somewhere in the grass,
a bus leaving.
I realize that it's been, outside, a bright hot day.

The Farm Woman Speaks

Winter has arrived, the winds scour this place.
Feeding the children broth,
I show them now, through the dull windows,
trees rocked by a cruel cough.

We can't take a bad year,
but the lino looks like an over-ripe banana:
there's no help pacing the floors.
Leaves panic with claws on the verandah

from those trees that boom all day. Usually
you don't notice the trees' noise until night,

4

but if you wake then, you'd swear the sea had come
crashing inland; that awful fright

passes as you realize
where you really are, and where we are
is with crops burnt by frost, the cows
eating dry cornstalks, with all of our care

about three children and a little money
sunken here; with the pasture grass
of a morning, in this worst season for years,
thick with crushed glass—.

Of a morning, I see him let the gates fall open.
The moon thaws. Wind floats bubbles
out of a magpie—and bears upon a salver
the croak of the crows.

He jerks in boots toward the shed,
buckets pulling at his neck.
A fig tree is clenched on the earth, and strain bulges
its tendons. The fences slop either side, gone slack.

There are still the times when he will turn to me.
At night, I drowse by the persimmons in the log,
and, first, he puts an arm around me—.
Only, those flames then feel like a striding flag.

"Scattered lights . . ."

Scattered lights,
one pub, and one garage.
Driving through

in the woodsmoke dusk.
A culvert
at the town limits;

the road goes on, straight,
fading. The flat
grey heath

disappearing close, on either side.
This blustery wind
brings rain—just

short hairs
on a barber's sheet,
marking the windscreen.

Morning

Feeding chickens, pollard scattered like wet sand.

They jump down stolidly from their roost
as an old sailor jumps
with wooden leg;
in there, underneath half a corrugated-iron tank,
open-ended.

I'm stepping around the bare black ground;
wire-netting propped
on lopped poles.
Moss about, bits
of brick poking through, and bones.
Rusted wrench
pressed into the ground, jaws open—
a tyrannosaurus head. Reeds.

In packing cases, one side gone, the eggs
in dry grass.
On this cold morning, they're warm, smooth:
Surprising stone

almost weightless.
Bent over;
at the side of my face, the silver
liquid paddocks, and steam.
My eyes and nose are damp, I see through my own smoke.

Finding the eggs, dry—the colour of dry sand.

Salvation Army Hostel

I'm woken up—and God knows
what's the time. It's
a woman screeching, over there
the other side of
the light-well.
I strained against the window-wire, tonight, and saw
the bottom, with rotting rag,
cardboard—a no-man's
greenish hole. And there's
evidently been rain,
surprisingly—the aftermath still
falling from a
broken gutter somewhere,
onto
that concrete
way down—
a clattering. No . . .
she's yelling at someone
on a floor above this who's

taking a piss, out his window—
It keeps on. He must have
got a flagon in
this place, and have his cock out through
the criss-cross
grille. A dripping
now, past me—turned over so's
to listen. I can almost see
his blind, bloated face up there
gasp.
No one else but that woman
seems awake. Who suddenly drags her window down.—
Both gone.
And I lie in the stiff, thin,
stencilled sheets,
again. Like an unresolved equation;
in this aperture.

17 Poems

A waterbird goes up
out of dead grass, its slow flight
water lapping.

The chair, made of frayed light,
speaks of absence
like half a carpenter's join.

Folding sacks
in the dim shed. From the house,
sound of crockery.

In the rock pool, grass
moves with the water. Violin bows
adagio.

Dusk. I go to scythe
under trees at the front gate.
Pale moths rising.

The rain: white grapes.
And this cobweb odour
of wet dust.

Putting a milk-bottle on the step,
a little tap water inside
reveals the moonlight in the same
frail quarter as this moon.

The back fence is falling,
or it's lifted within a Hokusai wave—
the morning glory vine.

In the lane, someone
walks back with a scrap of bush,
not glancing up, at dusk.

These ripe days,
the heat, the tenderness;
a white bathtub filled with green water,
leaves against the glass.

A few cars, way off
on the freeway, over wide fields—
a lost burst of tracer fire
through the bright afternoon.

On this peak, alone;
in the wind, it feels as if my shirt
is trying to go back.

9

Two swallows skim
a long verandah, over cane chairs;
bodysurfing the breeze.

Sultry night. The moon
is small and fuzzy, an aspirin
in a glass of water.

Chopping wood,
I strike about at mosquitoes
with the axe.

Smokestack, evening sky;
and the smoke, a woman's long hair,
who pauses underwater.

In the rain, a bedsheet pegged
unevenly on the sagging line.
It's there, patient and heavy as
a rhinoceros in whitewash.

Back There

A farmer in brittle morning
struggles with solid milk cans, his gasping
all around him—

Across the yard
of scarred
mud, the tangled branches
iron lace,
and a shed is going down sideways
under convolvulus.

There's moss
on the walls
one side of the house.
A rusty plough
is stranded like the horns of a
twisted neck,
out in the mouldy
grass.

And over the raw, stripped paddocks, up
on
the windy skyline,
children run,
capering
all about that huge nerve-end,
a bare tree;
flickering, black.

On Climbing the Stone Gate Peak
(Hsieh Ling-yün, AD 385-433)

In a floating gown, I have come among these promontories
     alone;
the path is struggling on like a wounded snake.
The crags above Stone Gate are piled one upon the other:
it seems as though they will topple from out of the rushing
     mist.
All about on ledges cling the twisted pines;
all over the rocks there is moss, like a discoloured snow.
I wander into a dark copse, which the late sun pierces,
and in this gloom, a pool of scarlet water.
The haunts of ape and deer have been left behind;
only a bird now cries out mournfully, in search of its mate.

I climb by caves where dripping water rings like crystal;
and leaves of dwarf bamboo are dripping.
It is because of a waterfall thrown down, beyond here, on
stones:
the splintering of a white jade staff.
That long pole of water goes on being shattered,
yet is no more diminished than Liu-hai with age.
Across the vibrating pool, a light smoke is windborne,
and drifts above me—the spirit of a great bird.
I climb again, breaking the cobwebs of mist;
vines are trailing from the cliffs beneath which I find my
way.
Then, coming from a crevasse, gaze on other mountains.
They are blue and green inks, allowed to run upon slanted
silk.
How could one live among such pinnacles, but with the
True Mind,
which asks for nothing, but is open to all that is?
These rugged peaks will not prolong one gentle
configuration,
and yet I find here strange flowers (that are struck like an
instrument).
Only one who knows Detachment, and lets his thoughts
grow fleeting,
could love these mountains, since his mind is not hampered
anywhere.

The Death of Ronald Ryan
(February 3, 1967)

In the crash
pigeons on the roof
whirr
up, clattering

of wings—
visible
to the pickets beyond
those walls, who
slowly
are
at that signal
turned
around. It's done.
Grey
as Lancashire,
deserted
iron galleries.
—A revolving like a punchbag.
The dusty skylights
receive
early thin yellow
sun.
The tower clock's
nine o'clock stroke,
clang
of the trap and
his mind went flying
in the sound—
and from such tensed
sling.
To echo?
What has been done?
Some birds settling down
later
along the way back.
—Hey, there's no air here
in this bag!
You don't want
to see me—
Those pigeons
in the gravel of the
roadside
are taking hasty steps, puffed

13

and
eyeing us side-
ways with
eyes trembling.

Within the Traveller's Eye

A late afternoon. From this passing train
one sees the forest.
It is like a cupboard, in some deserted room,
with its door ajar.

There has been rain. Now, so late, the sunlight reappears.
We are flying low, through these small country towns . . .

Morning glory vines grow over the wire fences
in the shape of huge snowdrifts.
Someone fat is leaning heavily on his verandah rail.

And those old pine trees in a loose main street,
where sparrows live like fleas.

We go above the mud and fallen light of an estuary;
a few birds rise.
The river, towards evening, is moving slowly
under a slow sky.

Seeing these small towns, there returns to mind
the life of an old woman—

It is those lavatories, out in the back yards
overgrown with paspalum;
a wet cardboard box, lying about;

the piles of weathered palings stacked on trestles;
a floor-cloth, that the dog has taken.

It seems there was always this shallow afternoon light.

Steep iron roofs, old wooden places;
they face each other on gravel side streets,
with rainwater ditches out of which the grass stands,
a ramp across to each.

There is a utility moving
behind tall roadside heads of grass,

a child's white apron.

A man is walking on the long shadows
of the telegraph poles, going for cigarettes and matches
to the shop.

I know those dim, unused sitting rooms:
faint gleam of lino
among the rugs, and everything in there as rounded
as Melba's bodice.
The fringes on everything.

All through such a house was the smell of boiled vegetables,
and there was something else
living amidst that odour—

it was the sexual hatreds, stored away
like china or cuff links,
and never spoken.
There only the daily second-best was used.

As daylight is turned low
in the grass, people by the kitchen windows,
or in the outside bathroom, at the end of a verandah,
can hear again the frogs

and crickets
begin, out in those flat, soggy paddocks.

But we have gone now miles beyond a town.
The shadow of the tallest mountain
in the valley wall

is lengthening over an empty plain of grass
we move across.

And it feels
this shadow is going to indicate, as though it were a finger,
a grave, lying open
somewhere here.

And you have to try to turn your face away.

The Pine

With a snow-cap
only
of needles;
aslant. And the lopped-off
branches of
various lengths
about its trunk.
The rhythm amongst these
such
a music, all
by chance.
Alone
in the back paddock
in the yellow grass.

Boarding House Poems

1

The landlord
standing on bare feet
saws
at the bread
in the middle of a Saturday
afternoon, to
a nasal
racing commentator's voice.
His wife
holding a cigarette
in the television room.
You go back
quietly on
the linoleum, and
the closing of
your
door.

2

Sound of traffic
outside, continuously
back and forth—
the table tennis
highway.
A sound
as if some kid
of an afternoon
is swinging viciously
right, and left,
cutting through the air
with a stick;
and a rapid bumping,
slapping noise

over the tar joins
in the concrete.
It's hot.
I lie on top of the bed
with a book.
A clock drips,
and the leaf shapes barely move
on the yellow blind.

3

Public Library
Putting a book up, moving on;
keeping hold of the one
pared volume.
Hushed,
starkly fluorescent-lit,
the air
dressed with dust.
A bald man
digs into his nose;
mustachioed man,
dog-like, in a moth-eaten overcoat; the
anxiously-peering woman.

4

Turning away
from the ladies' hairdressing salon
atmosphere
of the advertising agency—
going to work where
it's all
factories,
vacant lots, of weed and broken concrete,
terrace houses,

alleys. Down here
a light in the Italian corner shop
burns all day.
Anything feels better
for a while.
And one time
you find yourself in blunt real agreement
with someone—
that one of the other workers is officious;
"a bloody old woman".
The taste of comradeship.

5

Lunchtimes
you see
from a bank
above the hurricane wire
a schoolboy
soccer match:
the ball
trickling smoke
all about the dry grass.
The tall chimneys
above
trailing their smoke
one way.

6

Coming in, amongst the dark wood
of the hall
early, while it's still afternoon,
you notice
the calico-looking flowers, crowded
in a vase.
How they keep on hoping.

19

7

Wednesday, the dead, dark
and middle of the week—
hardly redeemed
by its being pay-day;
after putting aside the rent,
straight away this evening
the most urgent job,
the washing to the laundromat.
Reading a novel,
inattentive,
on the orange polythene chair;
parched smell
of dry-cleaning fluid,
and lifeless, dehydrated air
from spin-dryers.
During this hour, and more,
lots of times look up
and find her—
unloading bedsheets
that are like great lumps of dough
from a washing machine, or untangling
heat-blasted things,
holding the door against her side.
Intent profile
and the jeans stretched
tightly around, a
taut weight
in her shirt:
excitement
that rolls over in your stomach like
a dolphin.
And then, nothing else to do, but go,
as her air would indicate.
It's started to rain
lightly.
The rain comes undone
from a rail,

walking beside it home.
The rain is sliding
like a belt,
at an angle through the street light.
With both arms around
the large plastic bag of wash;
feeling it warm
against your body—
and the minute drops
cling
all over your face
and come stirring down, out of
your hair.

8

Rising like a clear moon,
on the wall
at the foot of my bed,
one picture—this photograph of
a Buddha;
an alert face, with a detachment like
the moon's,
with its
relentlessness.
"As Orpheus walked
amongst the forest, so you have passed
in this world:
a voice that might dispel
the beast in men."
Lying here
I'm reminded, once again,
that it is definitely
askew.

A Labourer

He goes out early, before work, half asleep,
webs of frost on the grass; wading
paspalum to the wood-heap,
a bone-smooth axe handle pointing at him. It lifts the block
on a corner of beetled, black
earth. The logs are like rolled roasts,
they tear apart on red-fibred meat. The axe squeaks out.
Lifting it—
the head pulls backwards—
now he sinks to where he is. And the new tile roofs
encroaching about
in the thin water of the sun;
the lavatories towards here, up the back yards.
Roosters scream
through iron, spurred timber
left stand. Bringing the axe down
bounces gong-blows off the ground, raises the crows;
forging off with rusted cries
into the steam. He takes an armful of the kindling
to drop in the box beside the stove,
and splinters hang
from a red, hieroglyphed hand—
These for the child, who's father to the man;
sitting-up, so reluctantly,
in the small mist of his breakfast.

"The Single Principle of Forms"

All day a storm has fermented. Now the clouds are
huge above the mountains.
A horse stands in the paddock and swings its wooden
face at the flies.
It stands with one hind-leg poised lightly by the
other, like the way a male ballet dancer stands.
Its muzzle soggy as the stump of a freshly-cut banana
palm.
And that coarse long tail makes you think of an
Indian, waiting with a tomahawk amongst the forest.
The horse trembles its flank in the heat, and now
lightning shudders—
A silverish lightning, over those great haunches of cloud.

Church Grounds

Bright Sunday at lunchtime
in the grimy suburb:
the presbytery's at prayers
or eating, and the nuns also—
I shortcut through
their schoolyard, down the steps
beside the church, onto
asphalt marked out
for basketball, in orange,
with the metal goals
swung down by the kids, the nets
torn and hanging like
stranded seaweed.
The garbage cans are strewn about

by children or
the stray dogs. Down here
under brick walls
(the colour of cold baked meat)
a flock of pigeons
walking. No one else around.
Pigeons pedal off in all
directions, eyes backwards—they
keep pecking
at the air in front of them
as they go. Tic, tic, tic.
If they're not
stabbing the earth, quelling every
speck, they're keeping on
with their demand,
their wanting, wanting—this peck
that's produced the pigeon—
into nothing;
it's their whole life.

21 Poems

Sanding the floorboards;
across the house, in a blank window,
hibiscus flowers.

The umbrella,
a crushed insect; in the sleet
on a drifting canal.

Sinking of autumn . . .
I've been getting by without you;
now, a touch of fear.

On the enamel dish, slice open
a pear;
rain hangs in the window gauze.

Late afternoon.
Clouds that might be Kilimanjaro
from the dry savanna.

Soaking in the hot bath;
on a radio somewhere
the time-pips.—Three o'clock.

Even leaves scraping
the concrete . . . I think that's
her step, again.

I get up and go to the window;
bright moonlight—
the sea is a glass that's brimming
under the tap.

Some children's voices,
a piano, in the hollow School of Arts.
In the alley, rain floating.

Long, wet verandah boards
with leaves blown in.
Where else could our souls live,
but on the earth?

Hot night; in the garden
I tighten the tap, it keeps dripping
on the brick. Mosquitoes come.

Stone jug filled
with milk, and two bubbles
like an igloo.

Passing on a train;
bedsheets borne out from a clothes-line
and the pasture-land.

Huge, glittering stars.
Looking up, out among the frogs'
croaking, croaking.

A porch with lattice;
green tendrils are moving
before the surf.

The new moon—
fallen out of its gown,
a white breast.

The rain, soft and everywhere,
becomes cricket calls
crackling, popping, in the loam.

Walking in high forest;
a swallow   blown away
from a crest of the trail.

In the city
the unexceptional night—
small change.

A drop hung,
indoors, from the tap's blunt
beak. A bird sings.

Burnt-out cornstalks askew
in the wet.
Standing hooded with a sack
amongst a battle's aftermath
long ago.

Credo

What shall we believe in? Here,
it's a stone

because you cannot think this away.
Or the polished table—

across it, light from the window falls.
Leaves outside
are moving, deep within this light.

"The nature of things is independent
of my will."

The Meatworks

Most of them worked around the slaughtering
out the back, where concrete gutters
crawled off
heavily, and the hot, fertilizer-thick,
sticky stench of blood
sent flies mad,
but I settled for one of the lowest-paid jobs, making mince
right the furthest end from those bellowing,
sloppy yards. Outside, the pigs' fear
made them mount one another
at the last minute. I stood all day
by a shaking metal box
that had a chute in, and a spout,
snatching steaks from a bin they kept refilling

pushing them through
arm-thick corkscrews, grinding around inside it, meat or
    not—
chomping, bloody mouth—
using a greasy stick
shaped into a penis.
When I grabbed it the first time
it slipped, slippery as soap, out of my hand,
in the machine
that gnawed it hysterically a few moments
louder and louder, then, shuddering, stopped;
fused every light in the shop.
Too soon to sack me—
it was the first thing I'd done.
For a while, I had to lug gutted pigs
white as swedes
and with straight stick tails
to the ice rooms, hang them by the hooves
on hooks—their dripping
solidified like candle-wax—or pack a long intestine
with sausage meat.
We got meat to take home—
bags of blood;
red plastic with the fat showing through.
We'd wash, then
out on the blue metal
towards town; but after sticking your hands all day
in snail-sheened flesh,
you found, around the nails, there was still blood.
I didn't usually take the meat.
I'd walk home on
the shiny, white-bruising beach, in mauve light,
past the town.
The beach, and those startling, storm-cloud mountains,
    high
beyond the furthest fibro houses, I'd come
to be with. (The only work
was at this Works.)—My wife
carried her sandals, in the sand and beach grass,

to meet me. I'd scoop up shell-grit
and scrub my hands,
treading about
through the icy ledges of the surf
as she came along. We said that working with meat was
    like
burning-off the live bush
and fertilizing with rottenness,
for this frail green money.
There was a flaw to the analogy
you felt, but one
I didn't look at, then—
the way those pigs stuck there, clinging onto each other.

Landscape

The river at its brim—
vast sweep
of ripples, full sailed in morning sun.

Clotted, drip-leafed gums
lean on the red
mud bank. Rickety log jetty
in socks
of oyster shells,
where milk cans stand.

The sawmill, a roof of rusty tin
on posts, over
shadow. The diagonal wooden
crane beam.

And dunes of sawdust lying about;
from somewhere there
a giant cigarette smoke.

The farmer, in felt hat, rides
a tractor, rakes up the dust—
lurches
on a wading animal. Huge embossed wheels
roll down.

An exhaust-pipe chimney
beside him: through those clear fumes
and heat, the mountains—
each a half-pitched
Big Top,
blue-black—
as if seen through a window
awash.
That stripe
of lacquered green cane.

Let off on the highway,
I climb down,
heaving a haversack
through smoky green bushes,
sulphur
bladey grass. The thrashing noise
behind. Insects everywhere, on the boil.
Stinking Roger—
hot, sweetish, fermenting smell.

And the river
here, in this mid-morning's
littered
with a whole street of
fallen plate-glass,
filled with
light.

The Cats

While my wife gets ready for work, I stay under the blankets on the couch, where I sleep when I've worked late.

The radio's muffled thumping, dishes' clatter. She goes, calling out about the shoe polish—swirl around of shoulderbag and hair, to smile again from the door.

Dressed, I walk in the back yard, and the autumn air is thin, the sky washed and shiny, like a squeaky windowpane.

These two camphor laurels, stirring back and forth, a sound like the edge of the surf. Their leaves glitter—the running water of the shallows.

And the shuddering of the expressway, above all the red tile roofs.

When I go around the front to collect the garbage can, there are cats about: I shout and stamp. They've been mating at night here, making a horrible noise, like a baby's desperate crying. It wakes my wife, who lost her child at birth.

I don't make her any promises, now, about that.

Every time I see the cats, I yell and bend to pick up a stone, and they leave with long stalking strides, bellies dragging.

A glass of orange juice. On the breakfast table, this folder of weak advertising puns.

I'm going to go to work late. I eat some toast, standing in the yard; the honey runs back on my hand.

Then cleaning up. Lifting the clothes from where I slept, I catch a glimpse out the door—the back part of a cat is ambling by, stealthy and confident. It walks like an Apache's horse.

To the Master, Dōgen Zenji
(1200-1253 AD)

Dōgen came in and sat on the wood platform;
all the people were gathered
like birds upon the lake.

After years, home from China,
and he had brought no scriptures; he showed them
empty hands.

This in Kyoto,
at someone-else's temple. He said, All that's important
is the ordinary things.

Making a fire
to boil the bathwater, pounding rice, pulling weeds
and knocking dirt from their roots,

or pouring tea—those blown scarves,
a moment, more beautiful than the drapery
in paintings by a master.

"It is this world
of the *dharmas* (the momentary particles)
that is the Diamond."

•

Dōgen received, they say, his first insight
from the old cook of some monastery
in China,

who was on the jetty
where they docked, who had come down
to buy mushrooms

among the rolled-up
straw sails, the fishnets, brocade litters,
and geese in baskets.

High sea-going junk,
shuffling and dipping
like an official.

Dōgen could see
an empty shoreline, the pinewood plank of the beach,
the mountains

far off
and dusty. Standing about
with his new smooth skull.

The horses' lumpy hooves clumped on those planks,
they arched their necks
and dipped their heads like swans,

manes blown about
like white threads from off
the falling breakers;

holding up their hooves as though they were tender,
the sea grabbing at
the timber below.

And the two Buddhists in all the shuffle got to bow.
The old man told him, Up there,
that place—

The monastery a cliff-face
in one of the shadowy hills.
My study is cooking;

no, not devotion. No,
no, not your sacred books (meaning Buddhism). And Dōgen,
irate—

he must have thought
who is this old prick, so ignorant
of the Law,

and it must have shown.
Son, I regret
that you haven't caught on

to where it is one discovers
the Original Nature
of the mind and things.

•

Dōgen said, Ideas
from reading, from people, from a personal bias,
toss them all out—

"discolourations".
You shall only discover by looking in
this momentary mind.

And said, "The Soto school
isn't one
of the entities in Buddhism—

don't even use such names."
The world's an incessant transformation, and to meditate
is awareness, with no

clinging to,
no working on, the mind.
It is a floating; ever-moving; "marvellous emptiness".

Only such a practice can bring aloofness
from the accidents, and appetites,
of life.

And upon this leaf one shall cross over
the stormy sea,
among the dragon-like waves.

Bright Day

The fantail is tying
loosely
a complex knot,
as if as an illustration,
about one spot
in the air

and then drawing it sharp;
yanked-tight
noose
on some frailer string—
the tangled line
in the sun
of a beetle, or other living thing;

throttling it.
It chops that end
short, and
this fantail, in its mantilla—
the swirling,
the blur—
goes off once more, taut;
not far

Again,
like some applause-igniting
artistry,
it flourishes a
variation
on that elaborate bow—
is adding, everywhere,
its satin
finishing touches to the morning.

Evening

In the bus, this silver pole is trickling from the hands that have held it.

The bus climbs back like a cockroach onto the Heights. As its gears grind down, people shift themselves, and the conversations fail.

They crush cigarette butts, or screw the ticket into stiff string for poking at their teeth. And with the window open, look out through the thick glass of their own expressions.

Ash falls like dandruff, smoke vanishes like someone's hair.

There is a woman with wax legs that are melting, running down in blue lumps. A man struggling to his feet drags cruelly at the cord.

Reading the race form or the lottery. A headline says someone-or-other's DEAD.

Tonight in these red brick villas, how many headaches like the heat lightning?

The moon shall press on all these roofs, dragging here a snail's path.

But after the heat of today, there'll be a breeze: the sound of a garden hose in the leaves outside. When people are lying down, beached in their chairs, with legs apart.

And they shall see the curtains set sail, of a sudden, as if for the New World.

24 Poems

A train is passing above;
in the pawnbroker's
we can't speak.

You forgot the flowers,
I have kept them in a jar of water.
It smells as if you're here.

Girl laughing in the 'phone,
sitting on the ledge, legs crossed.
Glass wriggles with rain.

I'm getting up later—
these stormy nights of autumn.
Sailboats on the lake.

4 a.m.; the Milky Way
blown along, high over the forest.
A truck changes down.

Rainy weather
with the light on all day.
Like waiting for someone.

In the locker room
a shower keeps on slapping . . .
the sodden newspaper.

Daytime movie;
and coming outside, it's dark.
I turn another way.

So hot, the sparrow looks ill,
sitting on the tap handle.

Freewheeling on a bike—
the butterflies of sunlight
all over me.

Lean in the wash-up, trying out a poem.
On the dark window, scratches of rain.

Sunday morning, late,
wandering to the bathroom,
it's filled with sunlight.

Hiking in the bush alone.
All afternoon, through branches,
vapour trail of a jet.

The pleasure of weeds:
to see them beneath the street-lights.

Weary, I tear open the shopping.
From newspaper waddles
on the table
                    like an irate duck
this melon.

I thought it was rain beginning,
sat up in the dark to listen—
it must have been falling leaves.

Drinks at a bubbler—
but that tear in his filthy trousers
hangs like a mouth.

The train's halted
nowhere. Small birds whirling up
from the dry grass.

Drunk last night; waking
with limbs scattered on the bed . . .
The shiny leaves move.

Sunken grave, iron,
come upon, trampling in long grass.
Rain-drop slipping down.

In the heat, dragging
myself about. For the first time
a nun is a person.

Feel my way
to the bathroom. Standing there,
clatter in the toilet bowl!

Dust grains on the glass door
in sunlight. Through there
a girl's wrists, about the vase.

A melon, overlooked
out in the muddy paddocks—
it's all right.

The Sawmill Shacks

The shacks are overgrown on the mountainside
we come rattling around
in Ted's bomb. A dirt road,
metal clang
under the car; the trail
to a waterfall.
Silent, chill
bush below,
the tree-tops tattered,
smoke-blue; high,
shot-to-pieces shapes against a frail
wintry sky. Halfway
on the cold
volcano, as steep

as sawdust
under a chute, once, in this dead
(oil-dirt and rusty cog)
crawled-through town.
At the top of the dry creek-bed of the street,
a furnace: rusted
cone with a round
tip, its sieve-like
smoke vent. An old Chev
timber truck's sunk
like a bullock down, almost gone,
blind.
The stores and shacks
are shingled weatherboard,
lines scored,
their boards curling
away. Huge, moist ferns
spout through the boardwalks and
fungus is spreading everywhere, like bright
dried apricot.

Just out, above the road,
the Community Hall,
weathered salmon-pink, slipping
through weed, some planks held by
one nail.
Inside,
boarded-up gloom, dust
in the door-beam
on the breathless floor,
furry.
A hollowness,
splattered with bird-lime. There's
a book on the floor, flaked
to rusty shale—
Baroness Orczy,
"property of
the C.W.A." And a Sunday school print

on the wall: a saint bestowing
rhetorical blessing,
smouldering, through the nicotine-coloured
stain.
A piano, with the seeming grin
of old bones:
caries, and the teeth's
enamel gone . . .

You hear the rudimentary violin,
the stamping boots,
and a sudden dog-like yelp;
tea cups scrape.
The whining, dogmatic women's voices,
and their squawks;
a bellowing, out of florid jowls. Those songs
of places they could hardly imagine:
Sacramento,
no doubt, and San Antonio,
and one would have been Phoenix . . .

Gladys, Clarrie, Madge and Arthur:
concerned about
the hint
of a slight—
with this mind that's too often like
a knocked-over
hive.
So little to do, anywhere here,
but resume;
their lives become a long time.
Women who'd cry
without finding any tears,
who startled themselves, wondering where this was;
those men
who did not pause at twilight,
whose solution was to put on
a snarl;

people the same as any—
blown away
out of a stony, slanted gap.
They have got lost again, somewhere.
On the mouth
a taste of pity, thinking of us.

The rafters are clotted with nests
and, treading about,
from inside the piano
a dead-animal stench. You have to push out,
under cobwebs
(the door-screech), stepping
jerkily in thin sun. And a crow lurches away
slides down
far off
we soar
over the vague blue mountainside . . .
How the tree-tops there
like wave crests
glint
in the last, reaching,
spatulate beams. And this huge dome

of air:
navy-blue, porous; the
blue of endless-
ness.
Inside your chest, you feel yourself arising—
Other mountains
far along from here, like skyscrapers
at dusk
with all of their lights out,
in the faint mist.
This opened-up
melon, of the evening.

Out here,
the long grasses

are swirled
loosely
like a buoy.
And now the stars,
the first few,
clear
as water
on a grass blade,
appearing
effortless
as
stars appear . . .

But we catch ourselves standing about.—It is
a sound of water
underneath the crashing of this
tethered avalanche—
the piled-up
heights of the forest—
everywhere.
And all that trickling water
seems an evil sound, in this place:
speaks of
black, icy leaf-mulch
that it sinks through; and of spreading over bald, slimy
     ground;
of the roots
standing out, furry, from frozen soil
like rib-cages;
a
deranged scrawl
of sharp-toothed lantana
where only it can pass—
in the enormous day-long gloom,
those torrential lines
of forest.

As if for a ballet,
all the light has fallen out of the sky,

and cold rears up,
the wind rises from the left.
Hard to see
the timber-getters' shacks,
each as lightless and empty,
as cast-off,
as a skull; staved-in.
This cold!
It reveals to you, like a disease, the shape of your bones.
Stumble down,
and now the headlights are swung solidly about
in a dank
cellar of leeches—
Feeling our way
through all four wheels of the car
out
into the long valley. And
dropping here

easily as an owl glides,
across these paddocks upholstered in powdery weeds—
The moon's
now fully risen,
afloat
in an immense fine spray
like perfume,
filling all the valley.
And one already said of nature
it is not "human-hearted"; except that, in men it is,
in some men.
Whatever is added to nature
nature's made.
Dimly you feel
out of what endless dissatisfactions we have come.

North Coast Town

Out beside the highway, first thing in the morning,
nothing much in my pockets but sand
from the beach. A Shell station (with their Men's locked),
a closed hamburger stand.

I washed at a tap down beside the changing sheds,
stepping about on mud. Through the wall
smell of the vandals' lavatory,
and an automatic chill flushing in the urinal.

Eat a floury apple, and stand about. At this kerb
sand crawls by, and palm fronds here
scrape dryly. Car after car now—it's like a boxer
warming-up with the heavy bag, spitting air.

A car slows and I chase it. Two hoods
going shooting. Tattoos and greasy Fifties pompadour.
Rev in High Street, drop their first can.
Plastic pennants on this distilled morning, everywhere;

a dog trotting, and someone hoses down a pavement;
our image flaps in shop fronts; smoking on
past the pink "Tropicana" motel (stucco, with sea shells);
the RSL, like a fancy-dress Inca; the "Coronation",

a warehouse picture show. We pass
bulldozed acres. The place is becoming chrome,
tile-facing, and plate-glass: they're making California.
Pass an Abo, not attempting to hitch, outside town.

The Great Buddha, Kamakura

Great Buddha,
a picture pinned-up behind the door;
all the swooping
loops of his robe;
the dust, twigs and berries,
sparrow droppings.
Crowds.
The Western clothes
wheeling prams, the shouts
of children
with those bright balloons
above their hands.
—Resentment,
idleness,
catching of another's eye,
acidic coins.
These families in the heat.
In every mind
there is the continual argument.
Great Buddha
as tall as the leaves,
in flak
of light and shadows.
Smile
elusive as the breeze there,
as a day that works out right.

GRASS SCRIPT

Late Ferry

The late ferry is leaving now;
I stay to watch
from the balcony, as it goes up onto
the huge dark harbour,

out beyond that narrow wood jetty;
the palm tree tops
make a sound like touches
of the brush on a snare drum

in the windy night. Going beyond
street lights' fluorescence
over the dark water, a ceaseless
activity, like chromosomes

uniting and dividing. And out beyond
the tomato stake patch
of the yachts, with their orange
lights; leaving this tuberous

small bay, for the city
across an empty dark. There, neon
redness trembles down in the water
as if into ice, and

the longer white lights
feel nervously about in the blackness,
towards here, like hands
after the light switch.

The ferry wades now into the broad
open harbour, to be lost soon
amongst a silver blizzard of light
swarming below the Bridge:

48

a Busby Berkeley spectacular
with thousands in frenzied, far-off
choreography, in their silver lamé,
the Bridge like a giant prop.

One does seem in a movie theatre:
that boat is small as a moth
wandering through the projector's beam,
seeing it float beneath the city.

I'll lose sight of the ferry soon—
I can see it while it's on darkness,
and it looks like honeycomb,
filled as it is with its yellow light.

The Name

He is a man getting on
in years,

who listens to racing
at the pub

when he finishes work
about 2.00.

Or he'll come straight back
sometimes

to the room. I can hear
he's lying down

again,
to use the name

of a woman
who has forgotten him.

Old House

In the long, windy grass
on the headland,
against a deep sea,
the closed wooden house, with its verandahs
and observatory.

The roller blinds are drawn;
a late sun throws
the shadow
of railing and bars, onto the weatherboards,
askew.

All that grass is rippling, the way hounds
undulate
on the scent. Out to sea
only the cold hoofprints of the light
are left. A white yacht.

The yacht appeared from amongst
the wrung grass
of the slope,
silently,
and is folded back now, along the coast.

The crack of their going-about,
and the cry
of a gull, echoed
in the bare verandah.
Down an institution's corridor, a white coat.

Poem to Kristina

1

Remembering a time, on sandy wheel tracks,
amongst all that sharp hot machinery, the bush—
Your flouncing, tired walk;
coming back, feet puffing up the dust,
carrying your sandals;
petulant, grizzling, laughing with me about it,
but still close to anger,
and knowing that I knew.
I can see myself trying to be humorous for you.

2

Among the rocks, I broke open
and persuaded you about your first oyster,
also. Talking like a cage full of birds, and
posing, gesturing, like a samurai,
to get your courage, you swallowed it
and with a scream leapt up
onto the sudden bracket of my arms,
and clung there wriggling your legs, and squealing,
and laughing out something. You liked it.

3

Your face, so often, ready to take offence;
defensive, hurt, if my eyes flickered
away while you talked all your unsure rush of talk.
Or else, you presented it with those hours of
barely any make-up. Posed, as playful and artificial
as photos of Marilyn. Which made me feel
your human "mirror
mirror on the wall"—a responsive mirror
of flesh for you to confirm, with my startled look,
what you'd found in the glass one.

4

At night, you wouldn't use the outdoor lavatory
last thing, for fear of spiders. And for fear
of the dark, you made me come outside
so you could pee. You bared your cream cheese
behind, beneath the clothes-line, and would remark
about all the tree of stars,
with your brown thighs splayed apart, like Havana cigars.

5

On grey days, out the kitchen window,
we watched the grey water moving by in the lake—
a crowd through turnstiles. Mooching about,
listening to our few records over and over;
in the half-light of the house, their combed Valentino sheen.
Making sandwiches at the sink, and putting on,
after enquiry, the Tim Buckley, or a Johnny Nash, or Van
    Morrison.
And sitting there, leaned together,
like two horses out in the yard in the rain.

6

Now I sit and look back. And we write sometimes;
we keep in touch, as they say.
I remember those times when I was happy
and didn't think I was. Strange, the way
only now I recognize it
as happiness. That that should be what happiness is like.
Too late, as people say.
It's true.—The worst is, you begin to suspect
there's to be realized, in life,
a homily as often
as we did not believe.

In the Bus

In the back of an old country bus, down a bitumen side
road through the floating rain. All the school kids dropped
off, we're going on to the next town; and now you can hear
the frying pan splutter underneath and the flap of wipers.

On a rattling wood bridge we slow to look at the yellow
creek rising: water coming over some usually dry large stones,
where there's foam like a curtain-end beating out of a window.

And through a paper mill forest—here every pine, I realize,
will have this shredded lank grey water all over it, delicately
as pollen upon a stamen.

Going on, to the shouted speculations of a couple of women,
a farm worker and the driver; the puddles in the aisle throwing
a straight punch on the corners; the steamy smell of wet
wool. The rubbed-off windows are again grey, and on their
outside is pebbled water, that trembles like the face of a
honeycomb covered with bees.

Although, there is the teeming green of the bush wherever a trickle of water has seeped in, and is moving down the glass like some small water-tufted animal that goes slowly along out there oblivious, keeping its head down all about the ground in the rain.

The Chair

Sitting out
a chair in the garden
morning sun
fine gravel among
outbreaks of flowering bush
ferns
a twisted surging white
log
lain in the open
the waterlily
stepping stones

Roof crackling in the heat
bird claws
all over it
this one-time farmhouse
a stain
like a grazed shinbone
on its long slide
tin

I see the grey-brown
fine bowled-over grass
in flat paddocks
fences
stitching it all

corroded smoky line of the bush
one coil
of the scaly river

And have to go back in
too hot
the chair's left standing
out
in the blazing yard
wooden
looming
in the sun

I can see it through these glass doors
in moving about
the hot shadowy house
getting up to spray flies
or to get a drink
the chair is standing its ground

And I want to sleep
I would like to be a seed
deep in the earth
I want
a dream of water
lying
in the mouth
a creek that rises
into a cave under the bank
and to wake at nightfall
when the autumn is already coming on
leaves falling

The chair will be standing outside still
the fallen leaves
upon it
it is like a working-man
bringing for me the basket
in his arms

Greyhounds

Bobbing of balloons
held by a string. On the tips of claws
click,
clickclick
softly. The pack
blown awry
easily, like a spread newspaper in
the elbowing wind.

Surely they are meant for some deviousness,
not that
full-pelt anxiety to kill.

Thus, they are such subtle animals:
an emblem
for the successful man.

—In the race
all obsequiousness or restraint gone;
they jack-knife up and down,
jockeying
upon a blast or slipstream
that's lifting them off their feet.

Whirling around under the lamps' roar.
They get their teeth out.

You meet them in the streets at night;
a soft flickering
again.
In the hands of preoccupied men
who fling aside the cigarette butts,
hurry and scheme;
who don't show them any love.

These dogs adapt
to anything, in the pursuit
of their own nature.

They lope right over the proffered
stains of other dogs.

I see them coming,
being given to walking about late;
and hear my footsteps
failing, as I approach, in this long street,
the lighted, empty
telephone box.

"The old wooden venetian blinds . . ."

The old wooden venetian blinds are closed. I put my case
down and open them with an arm that I can hardly raise.
The backyard, a scrawl of paspalum; just large enough for
its rusted rotary clothes hoist.

The shafts of light coming into the room are like the city's
escalators in rows, with this dust drifting along them . . .

Poem to My Father

Dear father, you were buried
in perfect summer weather.
Such a day
you would sit outdoors

and put your bad leg up
in its slipper,
and pretend not to like it there:
too crowded
on the porch, with the pot plants,
or too shady,
or too hot;
you would call out
to my mother and sister
and make them run;
you'd have your lunch brought
on a tray, with doilies
and frangipani,
presented
for you to fault.

Though, some found that day too hot,
and you could sympathize:
old-timers
from the RSL;
those red-faced
mates of yours, dabbing
with handkerchiefs
at hat-band welts,
the purple onion-root
in nostrils,
cheeks,
flaring, urgently as
heat lightning at night.

I told myself, your father
is in the rank grass,
who gave you body and soul.
That is why I've searched
anxiously
your face
propped on the hospital pillows—
for some trait

            like the corridor
of a dank hotel
        at the end of which is
                hung
a verandah, in the open.

I've found
        such fine bones
                in your face—
you have them yet.
        What one might only wish to keep
                of you, you keep,
also.
        In you, now signifying nothing;
                although
that chemistry was ineffectual,
        always—
                overcome
by some other gene
        or something infancy had done.
                That's all there is to say.

That's all.
        But everything you did once
                we thought against us.
The money you borrowed,
        won with
                and lost again.
All those days you went to get blind,
        so well turned out.
                The condemnation
in a haughty voice
        at every meal
                of my books, my hopeless maths,
my choice of sport.
        (I was the eldest
                and had to sit beside you.)
It didn't matter to you there was no

Rugby Union,
    I ought to be playing it.
I was letting you down.

Who was this
    thin-faced, hollow,
        neurasthenic devil,
with his ulcers,
    at the table with us?
        To whom everything was distasteful.
Mocking.
    How bad-tempered you looked
        after your close
fortnightly haircut.
    I could outrun you, and I needed to,
        by the time I was eleven.

And we ran out
    at night
        when it was past the time
you should be home—
    at our mother's intuition
        prodding
under the lantana
    along the road.
        We'd find you
with the bottles emptied
    that you, already drunk, had decided
        you were going to bring.
Once you began
    you'd keep on
        until the blessed, regular
Repat. Hospital internments.
    But the day after
        you would get up,
shave painfully, polish your shoes to righteousness,
    and walk in the house
        "looking for trouble";

an excuse for another
    departure,
        to spend the precious
TPI pension—
The Money.

I remember
    our pathetic pride
        to see you dressed again
and walking in the main street
    of that town
        as if you owned the place—
"Such a hide",
    my mother said; she would look angry,
        and almost smile.
We were those sun-browned,
    skinny,
        bare-foot, bike-riding
small animals
    whom you ignored.
        It didn't worry us, for long;
we ran wild;
    we were all right
        so long as you weren't around.

Some might have thought
    you wanted to play the rake,
        yet it was always
without panache—
    with no verve, no enjoyment,
        no gaiety,
that we could ever see.
    With a determined, thin-lipped
        selfishness.
What went wrong
    when you were young? It was nothing exceptional
        that I can find.
So, you will become now

in your children's lives,
        sometimes,
just the half-conscious, troubling
    sense of something
        we have forgotten to do,
or to bring
    along with us,
        if anything wants to remind us
of you.
    You have gone
        as if you were an illusion.

Although, my mother weeps.
    It is real;
        she loved you
when she could.
    Your second wife, she got religion
        and stayed.
What was going to happen
    to you
        otherwise?
She took in washing,
    worked as a cleaner,
        and got all of us by.
The closest I saw you together,
    the most affectionate,
        she was holding your hand
cutting the fingernails.
    You were embarrassed,
        hurrying her.
She wanted to play.
She was then past fifty.

Dear father,
    you did everything badly;
        the most
"difficult patient"
    in the nursing home.
        Poor man.

I cannot believe
     your wretchedness
          on all the occasions I recall.
If I think of you
     I'm horrified—I become obsessed
          with you. It is like
love.
     I am filled with pity.
          I want to live.

Pumpkins

What in novels is called "a grizzled stubble"
on these pumpkin leaves.
The leaves shuffle
as you wade amongst them, their bristles
rustling.
One is slowly stepping upon
egg shells,
pagodas of orange peel,
on heaps of tea slops.
And the pumpkin flower,
a big loud daffodil.
You push about darkness, parting the leaves.
A rooster is on this slope, also;
come to peck
outside, in the late afternoon.
It is putting down its spur
with care,
and its eye is flickering about.
The rooster is red
and lacquered as a Chinese box;
a golden hood
down to its shoulders, like a calyx, flexible

upon its body, as it pecks,
flicks,
flicks, and blinks,
pecks. I'm holding one foot up, looking for
somewhere
amongst this vine. And find
the pumpkin—
segmented like a peeled mandarin
or leather
on the back seat of a thirties tourer.
I break the stem
and lift the heavy, warped pumpkin,
just when the vine's become
too dark.
In between pink and yellow,
its orange tone
can be added easily to the sunset
that's been going on.
I put the pumpkin beneath my arm.
Like a bad painting, this magnificent sunset.

Looking After a Friend's House

I wake sometime towards daybreak,
hold apart
the curtains, propping myself up,
and can see the moon
setting.

It's down behind the stand
of distant bare trees—those torn bits
of flyscreen
tacked
onto sticks.

The moon is settling
quickly, the way an egg yolk
slides along
and off
a table top.

It shines across
these paddocks, with their dark
turned-over clods.
In some of the hollows, in the moonlight,
water lies.

I reach back and
press the light switch, to go on
reading. And read
until there glides up against me what seems
an icy cat.

Drab as goat's milk,
the first daylight. I hunch down, and feel myself
dissolving.
And next, sunlight is heavy on the quilt,
I am under all the dust-motes.

Now this light will be inside, shoved right through
the house, cycling down
onto linoleum.
And I hear the refrigerator starting-up again
in the empty kitchen.

"Smoke of logs . . ."

Smoke of logs and drifting rain out in the paddocks. Those rolling paddocks are long grey waves, far at sea, beneath this blowing rain. And the dark line of bush, a crowd of emigrants at the rail.

Afterwards

A photo of you
against the turmoil

towards the end of
the wedding day,

holding for your
young brother's snap-shot

his pocket money's
gift,

a
kitchen knife.

You smile,
so open-

faced, into his camera,
shining and

holding out
the gaudy

Woolworths
cello-fronted box.

Flushed and posing,
innocent.

This picture
that still can make me

catch my breath and
turn away

as if I saw my flesh
part

underneath a drawn
knife-blade.

Tropical Morning

I roll over and wake. The light
is like a divorce photograph. And a sharp
bird-note
pierces beneath the verandah's deep

frontal lobe. Sit up to face
the sky, an infinite
cruel calm. Trees in this place
feathered bones. And the cliff, a brute

relic, re-emerging over
tin roofs. This light, with its copious dust
swirling, burrows for cover
indoors. The underside of a crust,

one's sheet. Another alarmed call. That alert
sentry, a weapon in its face, was here:
it came in the verandah's slit,
and has leapt again on the swollen air.

The Visit

Blown onto the coast road, I go to see my mother,
unexpectedly.

I walk down the same dirt country street
with duffle bag,

and find her in the garden; her prolapsed belly.
She is grey—so grey.

Her hands, lined with the garden dirt,
fly to her face, and hair.

Straight away, she must think of something to eat.
On back steps, wintry sunlight gossip.

I play some old records. Where I left has grown over.
My brother comes for lunch

and on the quiet he tells me she is not so good.
She does become tired suddenly,

"because of the shock", and has to rest.
I wake her last thing,

late in the afternoon. I must be in Brisbane tomorrow;
must catch the bus. Her soft loose skin.

But I'll write. She says that she won't worry
now she's seen me. Reaching up.

I go out, to grab a book I remember I have left here,
find her sleeping again.

Flames and Dangling Wire

On a highway over the marshland.
Off to one side, the smoke of different fires in a row,
like fingers spread and dragged to smudge:
it is an always-burning dump.

Behind us, the city
driven like stakes into the earth.
A waterbird lifts above this swamp
as a turtle moves on the Galapagos shore.

We turn off down a gravel road,
approaching the dump. All the air wobbles
in some cheap mirror.
There is a fog over the hot sun.

Now the distant buildings are stencilled in the smoke.
And we come to a landscape of tin cans,
of cars like skulls,
that is rolling in its sand dune shapes.

Among these vast grey plastic sheets of heat,
shadowy figures
who seem engaged in identifying the dead—
they are the attendants, in overalls and goggles,

forking over rubbish on the dampened fires.
A sour smoke
is hauled out everywhere,
thin, like rope. And there are others moving—scavengers.

As in hell the devils
might pick about through our souls, for vestiges
of appetite
with which to stimulate themselves,

so these figures
seem to wander, disconsolate, with an eternity
in which to turn up
some peculiar sensation.

We get out and move about also.
The smell is huge,
blasting the mouth dry:
the tons of rotten newspaper, and great cuds of cloth . . .

And standing where I see the mirage of the city
I realize I am in the future.
This is how it shall be after men have gone.
It will be made of things that worked.

A labourer hoists an unidentifiable mulch
on his fork, throws it in the flame:
something flaps
like the rag held up in "The Raft of the *Medusa*".

We approach another, through the smoke,
and for a moment he seems that demon with the long barge
    pole.

—It is a man, wiping his eyes.
Someone who worked here would have to weep,

and so we speak. The rims beneath his eyes are wet
as an oyster, and red.
Knowing all that he does about us,
how can he avoid a hatred of men?

Going on, I notice an old radio, that spills
its dangling wire—
and I realize that somewhere the voices it received
are still travelling,

skidding away, riddled, around the arc of the universe;
and with them, the horse-laughs, and the Chopin
which was the sound of the curtains lifting,
one time, to a coast of light.

Old Man

In flannel singlet
bends at the table. Slowly

shakily
he prepares

the meal—how neatly
slicing

tomatoes and
cold meat, then

arranging them
rearranging them

on the plate,
breathing heavily.

The Calm

Early morning:
it grows light in the bedroom
but is still shadowy

because of the clouds
like quilting.
It is a cool, firm-fleshed

young morning,
the bird-song random and brief
as wind chimes.

The light makes strange corridors
in this polished, plain
wardrobe.

The sound of a train along
the mountain
quite clear, beyond the quiet town;

a train going through deep blue cuttings
in the rock
and among the blue trees.

The curtains here
long gowns, under which the feet of
the breeze

prance
their few steps and
slide back.

One could have the bedlight on
to read, but would miss
this smoke-

soft
change of light.
The leaves are stirring like something

in a calm sea.
I get up, pulling my pyjamas together,
see where the newspaper

has slid across the lawn.
A dark blue hose is coiled,
bright dandelions

beside it, drawn
around in the seed-tops
of the grass. All this, so vivid

on a grey spring morning.
I lie down
again, under the one frail

sheet; lie still
not thinking. Listening to the quietness.
And I hear someone else is up

moving about,
that now in the bathroom the tap
is running, like a wound.

The Swallows

A 100-yard square reservoir is sunk in the open field
amongst the long, wind-drawn grass.
Rusty hurricane wire
surrounds this wide place, and beyond it one sees

73

some blocks of flats
that are like computer cards.
All the grass that we are wading into is sat upon by the
     wind
at once, and then it straightens
as if to breathe
and goes down again, in a slightly different direction.
There are smoke stacks against a charcoal view,
and five great cooling towers, overlapping,
with pipe-smoke seeping across the lips of some.
A very tall antenna—a pure line—
is ruled up into another part of the sky:
a knife-blade, portioning
the vat of bluish, watery skim cheese.
And here, everywhere above the pale brown reservoir's
chipped water,
the swallows are flickering;
a large flock, that is like scratchings upon an old film
of the English town below.
Going closer, the swallows seem black scraps of paper that
     whirl and turn
over a bonfire.
Their rubbery wings
are like long, narrow fins, and they plane down on these
fast, twittering them alternately.
We flinch and duck—amused,
startled, at the way they have begun dive-bombing us.
Little pronged, sharp tails,
and porpoise-shaped bodies, splay-beaked.
They are bouncing and rebounding all about the air.
These juddering bats,
diving at us, continuously, and planing off.
And beyond them now, a Choral Vision—
the cathedral window strainings, through smoky air,
of late afternoon sun.
The sun is gathered into a bouquet of stage lights
on the English countryside, that is like a golf course,
on gas tanks, and on the cold tea

of the cramped river.
And these darkening swallow shapes
have been reduced, each, to a symbol—
they are just a quarter moon with an arrow crossing;
that symbol on many dozen
churned-about flags—stretched,
or snapping, or falling in the wind.
There is such an eloquent, fervent demonstration on this
     hilltop.
It's something ritualized and ancient
with exuberant life—
something, outside the museums, that can overcome
the sharp play
of the visitors' deflation.

14 Poems

White rowboat,
slowest wingbeat. A hotel window's
flower-patterned air.

Cold afternoon fields;
the lights of a roadside shop
fill the puddles.

Train on the embankment;
above the spread backs of marsh birds
a Sacred Heart twilight.

Figures racing to the surf;
they strike the silver water, crooked
as roots of ginger.

Mountainside dusk;
white flowers scattered through the bush,
milking-shed lights.

Archipelago of morning—
the clouds are dark purple sandbanks,
golden water among them.

The station master,
gazing across the wide, hot flats,
pours tea-leaves on the tracks.

Verandah rail
and above, a stripe of ocean.
The clouds' stage.

Drying her eyes,
come out on the hilltop street;
hiding in the wind.

Stopping by the highway
to piss. Against dawn, the foliage
of eucalypts, like rags.

At the cafeteria
a few people, and all the table-tops
in wide morning light.

In a window, early,
the city, across the harbour;
or stumps of a gully
in the smoky morning bush.

This torch beam
I feel with, through the pouring night,
is smoke.

Late afternoon trees;
a curved, empty highway. One side,
the rushing grass is lit
as if, somewhere,
a door has been left ajar.

Dharma Vehicle

1

Out of the reach of voices
in the wind.

Camping at a fibro shack
fishermen use—
swept with tea-tree branches, and washed down
with kerosene tins of
tank water.

Like banners raised,
all these eucalyptus saplings—
the straight trees.

A sea-breeze
over the grass headland, where fallen, white
branches swim;
leaves here
are shaken all the time,
shoes that run
on stone.

My bed
a pile of cut fern.

*

And the Pacific Ocean mornings

in windows rinsed with
wet handkerchief,
among the whitish-grey, ragged paperbarks—

that glint
all over,
in long shoals,
of translucent
scales.

At night,
lying by the fire
outdoors—seeming to lean above
moon and stars afloat.

The distant cannon
of the waves . . .

The paperbarks climb
slowly,
and are spreading out, like incense-smoke.

*

I read beneath the trees all day,
caught-up
with those old Chinese
who sought the right way to live, and found
one must adapt to nature,
to what is
outside our egotism;
who loved this earth.

"Here I am
gulping the stuff from the fountain
and willing to let it   (Lucretius)
trickle out of my mouth."

In India, the Buddhists

praised insensibility
to the world
("Doth not the Hindoo
lust after vacuity?");
but with Buddhism's arrival in China,
by the T'ang,
in the time of Hui-neng, the sixth
patriarch, there'd come
a complete reversal of such *dharma*—

There is the Other Shore,
it is here.

*

It is not reaching into any deep centre,
but to awaken the mind without fixing it anywhere.

A man who goes into trance
and has no thought or feeling   (Hui-neng)
surely is no better than a block of stone
or bit of wood.

But to know pleasure as pleasure
and pain as pain
and to keep the mind free from all attachment
is what's called No-Thought.

*

I turn out the lamp.
Leaves, twigs, berries falling
on the tin like rain
in the night.
—It was the monk
Fa Ch'an-ang, in China,
dying,

heard a squirrel screech
out on the moon-wet tiles, and who told them
"It's only this."

*

Only this.
A wide flat banana leaf,
wet green,
unbroken, leaning on
the glass.

The mother-of-pearl of a cloudy dawn.

2

How shall one continue
to confront every morning
this same face in the mirror?

Anxiously peering,
demanding—
such intolerable self-pity;

hysterical, and without decency.
Impossible marriage
with such a face, that eats up other people.

I do not want to be this sort of cripple
in the world any longer;
not for any of my excuses for being

to remain,
not for any of my possibilities.
I do not want to be what I am.

I'm woken here,
I would like simply to walk away.
And live without saying that I live,

without me
as the filament, the grains, the sedimentary content,
the matter to be taken into account.

And continue,
but without this continuing; certainly,
not to remain defender of such a proposition,

which, every next moment, life is going to contradict,
and with the back of its hand,
and with its fist.

*

When you are suffering
and you want to be free
of that which torments you,

it is not greed,
is it?
This is something more basic than

the calculations of thought.
And this is why I've felt
it's possible

to elude the mind,
whose confusion has continued
for too long.

The summer's almost gone.

3

The holymen whom Gautama sought-out in the forest—
torment of a leper—
knew about Transience,
as did Heraclitus, about this time,
but taught there is a soul,

81

Atman,
"I",
and that it's the same as the World-Soul, Brahman,
of abiding nature.
Gautama saw there is no cure for the Self
in such belief.

"I saw the thorn
that is piercing to the heart of men"—
and belief in the soul is part of its poison—
the thorn
is one's subjective desire,
to which a man clings above all,
tenacious like the shark
and as cruel—
"If this thorn is drawn out
one is calm and knows peace."

He could not find his relief among those *sannyasin*,
and so, went on alone;
staring in
where all the other's knees had failed them—
on the edge of the buffalo pasture
in blue smoke of moonlight,
in the wet grass,
with mud running on his body;
or among tree roots,
and there he saw the ragged wild flight
of the stars,
a particular night—
it was like,
as many others have said, since then,
"the bottom falling out
of the washtub",
or
"like flowers suddenly blooming
on withered trees".

*

"No God, no soul"—
It is all like a mountain river,
travelling very far, and very swiftly;
not for a moment does it cease to flow.
One thing disappears and determines what is arising,
and there is no unchanging substance
through all of this,
nothing to call permanent,
only Change.
That which is the substance of things
abides as nothing
and has nowhere
a nature of its own.
Its essential nature is Nothingness.

*

In Western thought, this recalls something that Engels said
in "Dialectics of Nature"—
that "motion is the mode of existence
of matter";
there is no form of matter that isn't in transformation
and therefore
no form that's an essence.
"Matter, as such",
Engels wrote, "is the pure creation of thought . . .
an abstraction";
matter only exists in particular forms.

So that these transient things, themselves, are what is
        Absolute;
these things
beneath the hand, and before the eye—
the wattle
lying on the wooden trestle,
pencils, some crockery,
books and papers, a river stone,
the dead flies and cobwebs
in the rusty gauze.

4

I am woken here when "the sun gets to its feet
shouting".
The sun takes a stride,
"wearing its waistband of human hair".
I go out, over the morning's copious small water,
never touched,
and the golden breath covers the dense forest and the
     mountains,
the paddocks below
that are streaked with dead trees.

I walk down a long slope
where the bush is cut far back on either side;
the early sky, so light,
has a feeling of
the first day up again after illness;
the dew is dashed in the grass,
blue,
gold, red; as you pass above,
it lights up, everywhere you walk.

From this hillside
I can see, around a solid, wind-levelled, slant mass of
     trees,
the ocean—
like silver foil
that's been crumpled and smoothed again.

And below me, dark timber,
with those topmost cauliflower-clumps of eucalyptus
scattered, opaque,
against the ocean light.
Beyond, there are banana plantations
right along, over the billowing hillslopes,
and a few tin roofs
lit-up like dangling water-drops.
I hear, faintly, a dog yap,

and can see blue smoke
that is staggering along the air a little way.

I go further down;
wade a lagoon of whisky-coloured grass
onto the dirt road (soaked
to the knees), and pass
a deserted schoolhouse, with its red iron roof and tank,
and tennis court
lying within wire netting; and now a flock
of parakeets
sweeps by—it banks
on the morning, dark lift of wings—is settling
everywhere.
They're leaping about amongst the trees, and some dip into
     the court,
vague behind wire
as if flying through mist—
wheel up again
catching the sun—their feathers then
the colours of that dew . . .

5

It was in China that men first could say
of this transitory world
it is Nirvana.

The Taoists had seen the universe is Self-Existent,
and that all particular things
spontaneously arise.

"If Heaven had produced its creatures on purpose
it would have taught them to love   (Wang Ch'ung)
and not to prey upon each other.

Rather, all things have come about through Transformation,
because they are one.
You do not find anything superior to things."

85

Such a universe was spoken of as a Great Furnace
in which all that is
shall burn.

It is a fire that consumes the fire, undiminished.
How could Heaven have pity for that fate
its nature brings about?

"Though all is in destruction and regeneration at once
there is tranquillity in this disturbance.   (Chuang-tzu)
Tranquillity in disturbance is called Perfection.

There are ten thousand things being transformed,
and the sage is transformed along with them
without difference, without end.

Therefore, his movements are effortless as water;
his stillness, deep like a mirror;
his response, an echo.

His rarefied condition makes him seem to disappear.
He accepts his body with pleasure,
forgetting life and death.

To him there is nothing in the world that is greater
than the tip of a hair
that grows in spring."

*

When something comes into existence
it is because of conditions that are favouring—

all-that-is, being interdependent,
combines to bring it forth,

and thus nature is good to man,
or at least, is more favourable than against him.

And everything appears, the Taoists said,
in dialectical relation—

it is like two stags
that lock horns close to the ground—a sound

of bamboos knocking together—
whose playful blood grows erect

in their veins: pushing
they manoeuvre

and stagger,
the dust arises

as all of these floating worlds.
On each world

and in every event of each
the same two stags contest.

And Lao-tzu, on leaving the Empire of Han,
at some vast age, to die—

riding on his buffalo
that was like a torrential rain—

wrote a poem to the people, and left it with the border
    guard:
that men should confess

it is the opposite of what we love
is good to us,

that it's only this weeping
which can make us glad.

*

The things of the earth
fill men with life
and swarm, like red corpuscles to a wound,
to do them good.
The earth feeds men aright;
the five grains are to feed them,
and the beans,
and the leaves for their soup;
and the water the same,
it goes down alive
inside men; and these fruits,
they feed men well.
And even Death—
the vinegar
that is found in the dish.
One ought to go out
into the forest and sun,
bathe in the streams and ocean,
and care for the body with oils
and comb the hair and decorate oneself
to sleep with another,
and join one's friends
in the grove of summer,
or beneath wide eaves
in dark weather, when the rain drips,
bringing wine.
And wander along the mountainside alone.
Because life is fleeting,
it is the breath of a bull in the wintry dusk.
Throwing away the self, "let us hasten
to enjoy this life".

6

The image of Buddha became a fat Chinaman
who was rolling on his haunches in a fallen-down robe,
twiddling as a fan
the end of a banana leaf,

with tits that wouldn't have looked out of place on a sow
and a laugh like a slice of watermelon—
to tear-up the conceptions of the mind.

Onto that way in harmony with nature there was joined
the sharp means of Release.
Before this, the Taoists were content with passivity,
and for discarding the self, most often
made do with wine.
The Emperor Wu-ti was first to hear the Unique Insight,
who asked of Bodhidharma,
define Buddhism.
Bodhidharma replied: Vast Emptiness.

*

Ma-chu got up onto the wood platform,
eased his legs in the Lotus,
laid aside his fan;
he started to trail smoking water on the green tea powder,
beating it with a whisk,
and looked over wet gravel, the heads of all the assembly,
between the darkness of wide, heavy doors,
to a lemon colour in the garden;
then he said to them, "There is no Buddhahood for you to
    attain;
cling to nothing, that is the Tao",
and signalled for the crack
of the woodblocks together, for them to leave;
and sipped from the bowl, alone.

*

And there was a Master, Hsuan-chien,
told his students, after they'd sat in the courtyard for many
    days,
prostrating themselves, to be taken in,
"Pull on your clothes of a morning

and work along the hillside with the others,
or rake the leaves,
until you hear the dinner drum;
eat your meals,
and go to the john when you have to—
That's all.
There's no transmigration for you to fear, no
Nirvana to achieve.
Just respond to all things
without getting caught—
Don't even hold on to your Non-Seeking as right.
There is no other wisdom to attain."

*

An afternoon rain
is drifting like sails of smoke
among these paperbark trees, about the shack;
it is the crumpling sound of cleaning up
cellophane wrap, close by,
and in one place, that green slap
of cow water.
"Sit straight, in Padmāsana, like a mountain,
keeping count of the breath, over and over,
so as not to touch your thought,
the eyes left open."
You cannot dwell anywhere.
Realizing, beyond the intellect, that "I" do not exist.

There is a soft, wet, vivid green,
a paddock, that rises
full as a breaker's first lifting,
now, after the cold steam;
and above it, struck by watery sun,
scaffolding tree-trunks, branch-beams, obliques, that shine
whitely, out of the black cumulus of bush.
And I hear rain tapping,
as if on canvas, from the guttering, and from where

a bird has skittered
all about this window, shaking the wet tree.

"A mind that's like a mirror,
in which things pass and leave no stain."

7

I'm coming back with a haversack from the shop;
a beach resort
miles off,
walking all the way at the water's edge
along the empty sand.

Those shops they have forgot
to wind.

The one street, an old faded print,
squints in the glare;
outshone
by the plate-glass sea.

And I climb, one after the other, over
the headlands, on rock,
in late afternoon,

looking out to where all the clambering, wilted,
flaring

Ocean

begins, of a sudden, its bellowing and stamping,
the lowering of its shoulders,
a smoke-spray
blowing from them.

The surf comes in as though alive and tearing free
from under the net of foam—

making its break
with the panicky, bounding gallop of some great animal up
hopeless
onto the slippery shore.

And all the time along the horizon
those clouds,
that are like mountains with cliffs and valleys, now,
in the last, stretched-out sun—
that dreaming, far-off,
impossible land.

Night comes
quickly, over the water, as if water
flowing into the space left by the withdrawing sun,
and foam spreads
flatly all around me, phosphorescent,
bubbling and crackling in crab-holes in the sand.

The waves flicker
like a book left in some vast, empty house,
to a noise of doors slamming.

I am weary and cold, by now.
No one about.
Only, across the rising moon's long beam,
a bird flies,
skimming the horns of the sea.

This long beach,
beneath the immense imagery of night
and the night-bird's croak,
keeps on disappearing into the mist and dark.

And at such times, "even in the mind of the enlightened
there arises sorrow",
so it's all right.

Telling the Beads

One drop is laid in each nasturtium leaf,
round as mercury,

and there are several on
every looped frond of the long flat grass;

these
clear sacs of plastic, tucked and full.

Plump, uncontained water,
precipitous,

held together by the air.
They are the most fragile particulars.

On grass that's loping everywhere,
in all the trajectories of a flea circus.

Thought balloons,
you infer

that I should fill each of you with its
apt word

which must be of a like transparency.
You are the mushrooms

conceived on the pure walls of the air;
anti-pebbles;

doodlings of a Botticellian elegance.
O claritas,

one thinks of lenses, floating upon each other,
dreamed by Spinoza

before a window full of sky,
all the Christians out of the house, and gone to church.

You are the digits of nature's prodigality.
You slip

on these stalks
as if one had become aware of the film

on strained eyes.
Presented on a febrifugal greenness;

someone who hadn't realized a need for refreshment
is made aware of an unventilated taste.

Looked at,
you offer hardly more than that.

This is authentic manna, it contains
no message and no promise,

only a momentary sustenance.
Run the drops from a stalk across your lip

they're lost
in the known juice of yourself, after the ungraspable

instant. Long-reputed but unresponsive
elixir.

Experiencing you, I see before me all the most refined
consolations of belief and thought.

Brushtail Possum

Thumps the water-tank
from out of the Gothic winter persimmon tree,
ticks like the start of rain
on tin
of the verandah
as we sit about after tea.

The banana leaves are shredded
like buckskin,
sway in night wind
against a closed window,
the fuel stove crackles,
the lamp-light an oily yellow.

We take some bread out;
a possum hung
over the sag of the guttering,
blackish-grey,
short-eared, snouted, anxious stare,
it swipes the bread with a human claw.

Eats it there;
nose pink and wet as a tongue,
tightly-packed fur
like moss. One eye is blue-white,
blind
from a twig or fight.

The whiskers wide-spread, like a spider's web.
The face twitching about
looks down
with its live eye
as with the one that's matching the moon,
against a salted sky.

Bellingen

bronze

linen tide

bronze

shadows

ibis

rowboat

farmlight

linen shadows

glide

Going Back, on a Hot Night

Now we are coming again towards a station;
out of the dark
countryside, the lights of a town,
beyond these sandy flats with their paperbark.

Over a hollow long metal bridge rumbles
the long train,
like a consignment of metal beer barrels
tumbled on concrete. And I see the small moon

above a dark sea, with the moonlight
in saucers, stacked-up,
teetering. Glimpsed as it reaches out
to mark the horizon. Now we almost stop;

creak forward. Street-light, palings. Archerville.
I know the Mail—
that I can stretch my legs a while
past these sacks and hampers, along the gravel.

I see a tea-leaf scrub, and the low moon again,
procession of one;
yellow kitchens; smoke; the pond-life of stars.
Through wide paddocks dart, like mice, a few cars.

I stand about. The frogs' hollow, ringing, regular
"clonk, clonk", from the scrub—
exactly the sound of a distant hammer
on framework. Going after some labouring job.

20 Poems

Waking at a station,
and across the blue-lit glass
that cold, far galaxy—
the rain.

The yachts—geese scattering
stately
in a flurry of harbour light.

A flag luxuriates:
those gestures of someone
taking a hot bath.

First daylight—
enough for the lacquer to hold
on the dresser top.

In a cheap hotel room
eating fruit—
it drips on the towel.

Across the level
eucalyptus forest, the sunlit
afternoon sea.

In a dark room
rustle of the long clothing
of the rain.

Torpid farmland, afternoon.
A windmill stirs
as bubbles break in buttermilk.

A car passing
in the night; headlights sweep
the kitchen dresser.

Sunlight-eaten, lace forest
over the mountain;
and far below, along dark trees,
a bird swings.

Wake startled
in the afternoon—
heavy footsteps.
Kids bouncing
a soccer ball.

Small hotel; a morning of rain.
Reading in bed, early,
by soapy yellow electric light.

On the darkness
one star. An insect caught
in something, struggling.

Signal box, somewhere;
a railway crossing sundown;
windy dunes . . .

Alone, eating watermelon;
a back porch.
Seeds taken from
the lips, like hair.

The summer night,
a meandering wake
in waterlilies.

Wild, dark sea, and rain
falling. Through the lighthouse beam
a great bird flies.

Struggle to cut
a slice—now the pumpkin brays
like a mule.

Hot wind,
long boards of the verandah;
a bare rope clothesline
fluttering its hairs.

A long twilight,
milky-grey. Raindrops on the window,
gulls on the grass.

Reflection

Evenings, there are people with no intention of buying
who stop to look through the fish shop glass—
men with noses that are soaked full of alcohol,
old women who speak to the hand-led children that pass.

Water runs down this window in clam-shell pattern.
Within, there's bounty, stainless fittings, clean light,
heaped prawns, and flounders white as ice cream,
the lairs' highway, the suburb in its mangrove night.

An Afternoon

stillness
the rowing boat

bumps
tethered bull-calf

blunt-nosed
knock

down the yard
on poles

light
painted on the river

a kettle's sound
tling

taken from
the tap

sleepy
of an afternoon

lighting the gas
a stadium

roars
and the leaves medicine-

drip
evidently

it's rained
shavings of water

the woodblock axe
strung

and chickens
pick

a bird springs
onto and off

twigs
a kid's mattress

the bird vibrates
away

and it flashes soon
in the river's

arm
darkening now

Scotland, Visitation

North of Glasgow, the train wound like a kite's tail,
in the first spring weather,
under the clambering, close horizon—
that skyline, semaphore,
The brown grass, at the time, with such perfected
bright enamel
for the sky, reminding us of Australia:
of deeply-rolling, open country out from Kyogle;
except for the crooked,
Japanese-scrawled, blackened pine trees,
instead of sparse eucalypts,
and a sudden tambourine-jangle of light through the beech
    leaves.
This after Glasgow, a place dull as Brisbane.
It is a landscape of great beauty, with no visual tradition—
even in Glasgow library
there seemed only two books of painting, both on
    Constructivism.
Yet, the Flemish blue of the lochs, like the Virgin's robe,
and the sudden, long hillsides
piebald in broken snow,
brilliant like a tropical sand.
Below the hills there were stiff, damp shadows,
pastel rocks, purplish-grey,
those red cattle that are like flood-wrack
hanging near stranded water,
and bulging low hills, bound down with stone walls like
    string.
We passed the upholstered sheep-lawns
reaching to a lawn-like sea,
and grey gables sleeping before a page of the Sound.
And then, neat English cars on the turf,
and the white lacquer and old stone of our ventilated sea
    town.
Like Richard Hannay,

we colonials were spoiled, for the spoiled southern home-
     country,
and had fled north. I walked all day
on the moor, alone,
with some genetic string plucked and vibrating within.
The only other moving thing,
except for a few sheep, that barely moved,
was the shadow of a bird, hung
different places on the grass—
although, in that bright sunlight, I could not find it above.
And just at dusk, there was a lone white bird, hurrying
in the distance
along dark water,
before the corroded facade of a pine forest.
So I turned back.
The black promontories, spiked and furry with trees,
drifted in the misty lochs.
And it was then that I could see, beyond them, in the
     furthest uplands,
dark, brutal-shouldered forms
amongst a cauldron-smoke . . .
I thought later of how, like children, men have done that
which is done to them. The apparent spirits
in the earth have taught us. Our fear,
and humiliation, bred hatred.
And yet the earth is Empty. It is innocent.
As everything, I thought, of that replete ground's cruel
     history,
was, in some last consideration, innocent.

The Dusk

A kangaroo is standing up, and dwindling like a plant
with a single bud.
Fur combed into a crest
along the inside length of its body,
a bow-wave
under slanted light, out in the harbour.

And its fine unlined face is held on the cool air;
a face in which you feel
the small thrust-forward teeth lying in the lower jaw,
grass-stained and sharp.

Standing beyond a wire fence, in weeds,
against the bush that is like a wandering smoke.

Mushroom-coloured,
and its white chest, the underside of a growing mushroom,
in the last daylight.

The tail is trailing heavily as a lizard lying concealed.

It turns its head like a mannequin
toward the fibro shack,
and holds the forepaws
as though offering to have them bound.

An old man pauses on a dirt path in his vegetable garden,
where a cabbage moth puppet-leaps and jiggles wildly
in the cooling sunbeams,
the bucket still swinging in his hand.

And the kangaroo settles down, pronged,
then lifts itself
carefully, like a package passed over from both arms—

The now curved-up tail is rocking gently counterweight
        behind
as it flits hunched
amongst the stumps and scrub, into the dusk.

The Estates

We drive on back roads,
across the hessian-coloured paddocks that are packed with
        dust.
The shade is left here of a few trees
like sprinkled water.

The tallest thing, high-tension lines,
these ledger rulings, among which the small clouds bloom
and vanish, like idle thoughts.
The mountains behind, a broken wall in the haze of collapse.

Rejoin the highway, where the bush is flapping in tatters.
Billboards grow wild. One,
a great arrow of sheet metal, is sticking up
obliquely, with the Lurex message HOMES—TURN HERE.

A net of blank, wide-open avenues
has been thrown over these cleared undulations,
and wooden frameworks stand, riddled with a dry brilliance,
on orange clay, beside rotary clothes hoists.

Completed, the houses are split-level, with chequered roofs,
garage doors wide as billboards, wrought iron curlicues
        about
great flag-stone patios,
cast-metal columns, and concrete flower troughs by the
        drive.

Now whole estates present the planes
of their picture windows and serviette-shaped gables,
one beyond the other, garnished with shrubberies and
    pencil pines,
against what seems here Perspex blue.

Ostentation is the estates' ugliness—
they're like those drawn-out American cars, with the fins
    and chrome.
And next, the town appears; all this biscuit-coloured brick,
the expansive gesturing.

Streets hang open. The lighting is elegant as dental
    instruments.
Flicker of a few walkers, and of many plastic flags
over vast concrete
of the service stations. A pneumatic blast of sun.

Lifting on, like a speedboat, down the highway.
Beside us, the TV aerials seem to make a thin steam
above the packed shapes in caravan parks—
as if the people there are slowly boiling in their figuring.

And you notice, too, the floodmarks of each year on houses
    near the river,
in this or another town, into the twilight of motels.
So now, you see how we have failed,
and you're beyond those lies about what profit has done.

THE SKYLIGHT

Dark Glasses

They lend a camera-lens intensity, and isolation,
in the sun-bathing heat,
to the blue hydrangeas across the lawn, whose each perfect
    dome
is made up
of unwavering jabs of mauve; and to a chipped laminate
cane stool, in between, that stands
palpable to sight
on the pencil-shaving grass.
The fence is coated with a small-leafed, dripping vine
like wallpaper:
each curlicue's edge
that sharply drawn. I turn my sight
on the equally sharp
definition of these potato chip scraps of bark
lifted on the grass,
above the tilt and scrabble
of ants, and feel myself trickle in the slowly
tightening press of the sun;
playing a breath-constricting, dangerous game.
The cicadas dilate and contract
as one, like fingers screeching down
plastic walls, in
crazy, rhythmic monotony. The sky
is an injection of maximum
blue, straight into the soul.
Supine, I prise myself up a little off the towel, to look
where she's standing at the hose,
beneath the verandah,
in the bottom of her bikini, drinking
and spraying at her daughter
behind the windows. She comes back cripple-
footed on the grass;
laughing and awry, so that water shakes either way
from her loose breasts, still white.

—I rotate my head down, a
few ratchets,
quickly, to see, above the dark glasses,
her breasts,
that are white as ice-cream
in her tan:
oiled and wet,
they look as though in syrup, or honey; each decorated
with a quince-coloured fruit.
And they feel,
I'd say, rather like
very fine, damp plastic bags do, when tightly packed with
      honey.

"In the early hours . . ."

In the early hours, I have come out to lean in the empty
corridor of the train, as it's crashing and lurching through
the night.

A liquefied dark scrub. And those paddocks where silverish-
grey mist is rising, slowly as a stirred moon dust.

The orange moon, like a basketball fumbled over waste
ground, is bouncing among the tops of a dark forest.

In the frosty, thick night a single farmhouse light floats
wetly as a flare.

I have lain awake in such a bed, and it has seemed to
me, also, it would be sufficient to be one of those carried
within this wind-borne sound . . .

(And I can remember, too, the mail train: a fine chain of
lights as I stood in the paddocks of a wintry dusk. Its sound
was that of wind through the swamp oaks.)

Motel Room

You keep on thinking of someone who woke here in the
     night,
lying still partly clothed amongst this bed,
when the television screen was a small animal, bundled-up,
shrill and squirming,
within a soiled white sheet;
and of how his mouth felt like a public place—
the phlegm, fumes and scraps
on the pavement of his tongue.
He couldn't remember which motel he was in—
the Sapphire, Blue Pacific, Palm Terrace, or Shangri-la.
The semi-trailers were meat-grinding
outside on the highway, as now;
getting down into the gristle and the bone
just here. He lifted himself, to wallow after the lavatory,
clothes twisted all over him,
and noticed how the things that he'd dropped everywhere
didn't change the look of no-one's place.
He made it back, onto the bed. Near this red lampshade
whisky left in its bottle
would have looked like petrol. And he raised his head,
again, to feel about
through the coverlet, and to sniff at this chewing-gum
wad of pillow—and fell back,
relieved if he could remember
at least there hadn't been a girl in here, that night.

On Contradictions

The black swan, drifting,
suggests a cartoon
about a Victorian lady,

being all refinement and propriety, with
a bustle.
Yet, on land,

it is at once a lurching
tough—the whole body
like shoulders;

it keeps doubling back,
then stretching-out, flexing,
the threatening

length of neck;
its mussel-shell beak, clacking,
drips;

a leathery
slap on the stones,
and hissing.

But it leaves
along the water, and now
again

is calm as a paddle-
wheeler, on some idle
pleasure course.

With millinery's most extravagant
bouquet—
the tail-feathers,

that are each curled inwards
fluffily
from the sides.

These live feathers have all
the ashen colour,
the tremor, and frailty,

of layers of a newspaper
burning
in a daylight, clear flame.

Walking in an American Wood

The moist deer woods seem sliding down, to one side of the
    railway line;
on the other is the slate Ohio; and beyond,
continuous factories, black and hieroglyphic-square,
through a feather-brushed drizzle, at dawn.
From the long nozzles of those recurrent chimneys is torn,
in bursts, a heavy vermilion flame,
rolling sideways, heavily as lava,
and the grey sky beats and crumples, over there, as though
    a pounded drum.

The eye of Osiris, where a bough is missing,
on the tooled leather of a silver birch, as I turn into the
    woods, before
a stack of dead cars,
and old houses on the outskirts of town, maple-splattered.
The pretence at innocence of an American architecture:
child-drawn, blocky, in clapboard, with wide-eyed windows,
    and simple steep roof.

Cars, long as crocodiles, are slewed up and sleeping, as yet,
on the bank before each door, and the television aerials are
    packed together
like waiting cattle-prods.
There is no more innocence here
than there's sincerity in all that talk about you're welcome
    and having a nice day.
Americans seem to believe you may have to eat or be eaten,
    and therefore
the complementary, frightened insistence on sociability.
I can make out a bike tube and cardboard boxes flung into
    the branches
above someone's yard, and wet newspaper and bits of
    automobile lying about.
In another yard, a half-sized statue of Jesus,
with downward, open arms, is looking toward the house;
and, as always, an American flag, big as a double bed-sheet,
    on a pole from someone's window.

Inside the woods are stiff little ferns, coffee-dusted with
    spore,
all about the steep, leaf-mulch ground. I climb through
    fallen sticks.
Left-over snow lies between roots and behind large rocks,
    in heaps of wet salt.
From the hilltop, I look back, among trunks, onto the river,
that's moving like poured treacle,
the flat folds of its pouring shown-up by sideways light.
The mist is rising eerily as a flying saucer, from the further,
    river-bound woodland.

I walk on, going downhill a long way. Branches slant right
    to the ground, like eaves
with many slates missing, making irregular, crooked, long
    openings.
Rising steam all through these sodden woods, and
    occasional lime-coloured lit undergrowth.

Sometimes I see another ridge, across the valley; the pine
    trees there the shape of a pine cone.
Mostly, all the dimensions are starred with leaves.

The slope levelling out, I climb over rocks, in the open,
toward a few older pines. These are an almost upright volley
    of spears,
landed together. Or they could seem abandoned teepee
    poles,
with some dangling feathers, in a slow wet smoke.
There are long projections drawn against their straight
    edges
through the sunlit mist. I sit to watch
light that's coming around them grow, burning away at one
    side of this overlapping stand.

Then, further on, black trunks against the lake—their long
    dry laterals whiskered like tap roots.
I come to the brown sand of the shore.
The little matted sticks and stranded froth remind me of a
    cocoon.
Along the open ground is old snow, the palest mauve,
    strewn thinly as fertiliser.
A cold watery breath climbs
through the air and through the bones of one's head;
it is refined into light, fleeing upward, becoming frailer and
    frailer.
The lake's glare and insubstantiality is dissatisfying,
    throughout the face, and in the throat, and the body . . .
I don't really know why I've come here, looking outwards
    into light,
nor do I bother to remember, but it feels now as if some-
    thing that's in me
will have to keep onward in this way, walking barefoot
    through the stars.

Travels *en Famille*

She began at once to use the train compartment
as though it were a room at home—
we'd arrived in our hammered, canine furs,
along the platform, through the rain,

and she hung the child's bright socks,
our overcoats and scarves on anything
that seemed a hook. With her best smile
which stayed there, like a transfer.

Two old women, under rugs, were cackling
their uncertainty. The man was cornered
behind a newspaper like a dented visor.
She dried the child's feet on her tartan skirt.

How "embarrassing".—I could peel open my book,
as usual. Schoolgirls were grinning through
a glass partition over the women's heads;
they tried their winking on me, and then wrote

something in fog along windows of the corridor
to squeal about, and at once rub off
for one another, aghast. The train jerked
as if given a great kick, and started running

almost at once above an open countryside.
A photograph of assorted river gravel
montaged on one of sodden, moss-bright fields.
Everything creaked like a soldier's gaiters.

The electric light, warm butter; and our coats
stirring thickly their steamy shadows around.
She read out the child's story, and we all laughed.
Beside us, a wall in two equal shades—

brown or green earth, and a mauve-grey sky.
A few trees at the fields' edge, as on a shelf,
like old pieces of steel *art nouveau*, their foliage
all the shapes of Japanese fans. I thought

a perfect moment, but then forgot about it.
We came to a small, flat town lying in the rain
and through its empty streets a sunset light appeared
shining on the sides of wet wooden houses.

The Garden

Butterflies, mandrills
consort with the orchids, and

beyond them, old dishrags
hung from the steam-pipes;

the trees in their hooks hold
a plexus, the vines.

Outside these wet palisades
grass swings open

where the lion kills, a roundhouse
from a gloveful of knives.

The lion drips in head-dress
and the sun, white as lime,

half-risen through Spade-shapes,
echoes the lion form.

—Man comes, and such a universe
grows conscious of itself.

Smoke

As if through a slanted blind,
the sun is made shafts among the immense rungs
of a Moreton Bay fig—
it comes sliding between that Gaudi-like, visceral
    architecture;
a slow,
egg-thickened, steamy
mixture, precisely-sliced and,
in rows, gently conveyor-belted down.
I watch across a road of
cattle-race traffic, and above the wall.

Over there, a gardener is at work:
his leaf-smoke
only visible within the slatted sun.
Discontinuously, smoke rises
and rears back, slides downward along itself, and winds
about, is gathered-up again, swelling into vast Chinese
    dragon sinuosities.
And, calmly, it seems giving birth; it keeps wavering and
    shredding,
then remerging, within the one great shape, like Taoist
    water symbology—
above all the interpenetrating, harsh lunging past here.

I'm waiting around beside a shop window's deep pool;
looking in sideways, I watch the people—
the threshings and winnowings of the city—
come right up and pass me blindly; leading with their faces
into their lives.
By turning to either side, I see
in the panels of sunlight across the way, or in this glass,
either the eternal process, as it has been stylised and
    revealed,
or its particulars,
that are like smoke.

Daybreak

Waking at three in the morning
the mind lies passive to sorrow;
this is the hour when the tides are turning
and when the invalids die.

And maybe at Petersham, soon,
the Greek woman who looked so ill, like a crow
in cold sago pudding, will board another early train,
on her way to cook or clean.

I remember our brains shall be the gum
in the tops of grass. And how we are leading in
a Dixie chorus—the tuba, which is the sow's happiness;
a trombone with its penis luxuriance.

Last night, I dreamt of the Rosenbergs,
walking in pine resin, in their "ideal marriage",
who have smelled themselves burn—their son was slugging
a ball, against a tin fence and the radio.

And of Commodore Perry, exemplar to Americans. For him,
ten thousand bodies of tar, in Hiroshima.
Gum had caught at someone's foot, who was walking in
   New York.
This frail light, strung with a chair-back . . .

I lie here and think how in the forest
dew-webs and globules among the highest twigs
are touched by dawn; pronged light,
as through a paint-coated, shattered glass.

Vaseline sunlight is over all the bush.
The steamy grass-tatters writhe as though a fire in plastic
   sheets.
Linear racket among willow and swamp-oak:
those wind-propellors, ratchets, corks out of bottles.

And the birds—a cutting of keys;
an emery-paper cleansing of swords; creaking
cogs and shafts, that ring little hammers;
a whole workshop—saw and file and craftsman's snips.

I imagine, in this city, sandstone granules clinging
to a crumbling, dishcloth-coloured wall.
Faint steam of cats' piss in that broken yard.
White sheets are held above there on a pole—

lightly stirring, with a late sleeper's sighs
and light eructations. They tug like soap-bubbles to set
    forth,
or decline into runnelled snow. White
again, with a whiteness we have made our own—

that I see as women's. Sheets like a perfect
fluffy pudding top, or snow within a flower-bed's
wire border—all about, the paths swept clean,
as a woman fingers flour off the dresser.

The Canoe

a pod
for the hand

is the canoe in
the mind

like a hammock
this dialectic

of the soporific
and cautious

119

it is tandem skiing
but we

are launched

trees fallen in
the river

steep
from the bank

steeping

the dawn's
grey weather

in the black boughs
bits

of pink and lemon
brightening

like watered
sherbet

the tide
is tightly stretched

this first
sunlit passage

a bee-swarm

the curled leaves
carried

high
and lightly

processional
into deep shade

silence

the whip bird's
long
smoothly-peeled

call

that breaks off
wetly

green
overhang

the high-lifted
twigs
and dust

membranous
water

now the river is
a sunlit
empty plaza

on the far shore
the tree-line
burned away
by glare

a forest highway

and we
lone refugees
with
a perambulator

cobalt sky

the bush is like
overgrown weeds
the cliffs
an orange clay

folded
duck's body
gliding

duck-breasted
swivel

the forest slopes
built
of stacked-up
tree clumps

dead trees
are scratches
down the mountain-face

on a smoky dark
glassiness

and the river drops
downhill
of a sudden
takes

rotored flight

straps tight
the chest

a wild bumping-around
aeroplane

lots of
shoving-off
off

off

we try

and then running out on
roller-skates

now
creeping through

the sleeping jaws of
dark pools
under cliffs

in crow-calling
silence

by late afternoon
a grey
marshland

where the river gives
itself away

in the face of the high
long silver
of the sea

back yards
along these slopes
with the wash
flying

a rusted chassis on
a mud bank

the mangroves
collapsed
footballers' scrum
in blue mud

caravan parks

dogs
and kids yelling

we land in
the estuary
a small town's
marina

and walk through
the summer dust

paddocks
above the sea

into town
to a restaurant table

in the dusk
watching

the lights of the ships
going by

The Sea-Shell

White as crockery,
it stands on the ledge of the long verandah window
in a white plank wall.

The trellis-lights—
negative, scrap shapes—are swung in here stiffly
as torch beams.

The shell is a lifting spinnaker.
And close-up, there are patterns in beige,
similar to a feather's.

The shell is wound
the same as pastry, and it has that same decorative
ruffled edging.

Coloured lead inserts in these bare windows.
Vine-patterns are stirring. Conifers,
bird movements. A Sunday.

The sound in the shell
is that of the whole Order at their evening meal,
along dim passages, behind doors.

The shell is cool, remote;
its shape causes a peristalsis in your palm,
it is breast-tipped.

Closed, adamant shell—
you think of some girl, who has been waited for here;
who's come, at last, from church;

who is received in her cool,
coiffured whiteness. Like the shell,
underneath her that dark passage, and damp smell.

125

"The best place . . ."

The best place to watch the rain.
is from the window of an apartment building,
on the third floor,
looking across an empty sports field, at night.
Someone should have left those tall sodium lights on,
faintly lighting the rugby goals, in a real storm.
And there should be taller buildings about
with a few of their orange and yellow windows still burning,
balanced on blackness, in asymmetrical pattern.
By this light you'll see,
caught in a long drawn-out pleasure, the vast collapse
and sifting away of a whole mountain-stack
of new slippery straw—
the bleached silver, and frail pliant gold,
whirling off.
Or the rain is a headful of blond, loose hair
struck by wind,
flaring out, and drawn upon—as stirring as if
that's actually what you saw.
Growing heavier, the rain can seem not a rushing down at
    all,
in some lit places,
but a rapid oscillation, a flicker,
maintaining itself in mid-air.
The night as filled with rain as a plank with splinters.
Eventually, you turn inside, the long window left bared its
    full length,
and on a table is the typewriter, and the sawn block of
    white paper,
one sheet a curving grass-blade.
To the side in this room, in a smaller but similarly brazen
    window,
a tree-top is plastering,
thumping and twisting itself about, like some enthusiastic
    postal clerk.

You sit down to the pleasure of writing when there is
    nothing that has to be written—
no article or review required; no editor
makes his pills ineffectual tonight
by chewing them with your name.
The desk lamp
curves its shadow across
all the shelved books, and they become
a crowd canopied in that vast South American football
    stadium,
whose voices now, in the midst of play,
you can no longer hear.
You're alone, the night before you.
The rain overwhelms itself outside. It is happiness.

On Politics

1

The idea most important to socialism
has been forgotten
in the title of an essay
that Shelley didn't live to write:
"A Proposal for Government
by Means of a System of Juries."

2

The experts may only advise
since it is we who have to endure,
and disprove them, in our bodies.

3

I have envisioned, as poets say,
a completely different kind of Party—
one that imposes nothing
but that helps induce, in everything,
self-management; and that would act thereafter
only as a judiciary, to maintain it.

4

It is terribly simple:
all men have an equality
because they all can suffer.

5

As men aren't equally intelligent or imaginative
nor are they equally virtuous,
which Anarchism would require.

6

One's touch with things, I have seen, is the same
as one's touch with other people.

7

Our vision of nature and of society is one.

8

If what is produced were agreed upon
with consumer councils, then each enterprise might reach
its social goal
democratically, through self-discipline.

9

There is one movement, which seeks to overcome
God, the State, and the Self.

10

An ineluctable delight
when the rooster, with its Nietzschean commission,
becomes fluff in the breeze
on the blade of an axe.

Bondi

The waves are a shoal of white fins, in the end of every
    downhill street,
and along the streets are stacked blunt-faced blocks of flats:
big, plastery, peeling buildings, in cream, with art deco
    curves and angles.
Behind this, for a thousand acres, the buckled suburbs of
    dark brick.
Curtains trail outwards on the heat, and a smell of gas leaks,
above singed grass in tiny yards, grey palings, chlorine-
    blue hydrangeas,
gas pipes like creepers over walls.
There are garbage bins left lying about, empty milk bottles
    on marble steps,
always snail-dribble across the concrete, to the crushed snail
    shells.
The sun trundles around and around, amongst its flapping
    fire.
In the longest street, out toward the cave-in on the head-
    land, is a children's park,

where, through empty swings, with their oversized hot
  chains, the surf swings.
Out here are callow home units of pale brick, fenestrated as
  that rock face
below the cliff's edge they're built upon.
Beyond a last railing, the sea throws over and spreads its
  crocheted cloth
across the rock table, and (something you can't watch for
  long—it is like madness)
draws it off once again.
Around at the beach-front, rattling fun parlours, discos and
  milk-bars, the sign-painting
lurid as tattoos, thickly over them.
Cars are tilted along all the gutters, strung together closely
  as caterpillars,
in the colours of children's sweets. The grit settles, coating
windscreens and duco; vinyl seats bake in the sun,
and that smell will sicken the overwrought children in the
  late afternoon, going home.
All day these headlands lie spread apart to the pleasurable,
  treacherous elements.
The place seems scoured by weather of every other ideal.
But then, a white yacht will appear in the ultramarine
  passage, an icon
of perfect adaptation, and the people along the sand,
as though in a grandstand, or those wading out
through the low waves towards it, seem all of them every-
  where over this
like walking moths, that fan its easy passage with their
  wings.
It goes wandering on midway in the spectrum of blue before
  them, in the garment of serenity.
This is the only sort of vision we shall have, and it costs
  money,
and therefore Bondi is lying crammed together, obtuse, with
  barely a tree, behind us—
Every cent is firstly for the secure mechanisms of comfort.
It is not pleasure, to be exact, but its appropriation. And not
  mindlessness, but the mind.

For at the beach, so much that is nature can be seen to have
    been called
into the one procession of decay. Flesh become crude and
    brief
as figures shaped out of beach sand. So many of these
    people
look as though used like Bondi grit, with its scraps and
    butts and matchsticks.
Still, the young girls are loping on the sea-front, who
    secretly
amaze themselves with an easy skill they've found—
who can swing their breasts and all the shapes that are
    surging on their bodies
as if the drum majorettes for this parade.
At dusk, the parking spaces above the sea have emptied
and sand blows along the bitumen like smoke.
The garbage bins on posts are steep in their slipping litter.
And the gulls, that run and screech and scatter each other
    amongst it, never make
contented noises—are scrabbling constantly;
only sometimes one of them is carried off by the wind,
    down the bay, and it goes along
on its outriggers, smoothly; beautiful, particularly in the
    dusk,
when it flows away as smoothly, sideways, as the running
    shallows—
its whiteness, that is picked up by the whiteness of a wave's
    single wingbeat
out there on the deep-mauve water, creating a vast space.

The Poem

The paddocks there are so wide open
she says you always feel
that the lid has been left off everything.
It's all gone hard and stale.

The children have to stay in the shade;
they hang on the verandah,
and the game they fight about is discovering
a demand upon her.

On the backs of her hands, in this light, open
small, dry screams.
She is bringing in the sunlit bed-clothes,
placing together the seams.

Sheets still pegged she takes into her fist,
and stands inhaling each one:
taut with air, white as a heron in the moonlight.
This, which she has done.

A Country Town

It was the sort of town where there is always an empty
    block of land
on the main street.
I was there one Sunday in autumn
and I saw through this gap how the afternoon above the
    hills was growing white
and was broken with swallows, insect-dancing.

Above that, the light had become white burgundy, and
    above that, all at once, indigo
and waiting for the first damp star.
The deep block where I stood was fenced with rusty,
    freehand lines of wire
and carried some old foundations,
hoops of thorny vine bowled in among them,
and a concrete slab, that had once been the bathroom floor,
now littered with finely-broken bottles.
Down at the back there was wood-smoke, above the
    galvanised roofs of another street,
and a few bare willows, in a tangle
like untidy basket work.
I watched a cow grazing in the shadows, on spongy mounds
    of grass,
an old bathtub tilted for its water trough.
This block was almost at one end in a street of deep
    awnings; at the other was the pub,
where local workmen, all timber-getters, sat
giving nothing away to each other, the loved undulation of
    a glass
felt by the cleft at the end of each arm, for hour after hour.
I'd listened a while, then come outside with my drink, into
    the freshly peeled twilight,
to the sound of a car, a dog's bark,
the shouts of a few kids
who pedalled in great bounds, beneath the level of their
    bike seats,
circling when the street became a road again.
A flying fox twitched overhead
like something caught alive on a stick (a country pleasure);
    and some midges
were moving together,
bouncing up and down, left and right, a bit ragged
but always in formation, as though being shaken around
    inside an invisible box.
I turned to the empty block, then,
and noticed in the last of the daylight a crooked tap

133

within a surge of grass, almost secretive, and the way it kept
    dripping
fast—unreasonably fast.
I was staring, as if through a keyhole.
That tap seemed frightening, and indecent, having gone on
    how long unnoticed there, dripping fast,
fast, yet silently,
with a hammer's little finalising silver blows.

Sketch of the Harbour

The long, wet trajectory of the ferry's railing
widely outswinging
is safely caught in my hand.

And I watch a yacht that is coasting by,
at its bow the fuming
of a champagne bottle's lip.

All about on the harbour the yachts are slowly waltzing,
or in close-up
their ecstatic geometry.

Light fragments crackling above the suburbs and water,
whitely, as from a welder's torch,
on a soap-white day.

In the shadow of the ferry, the oily, dense water
is flexile, striated
as launching muscles.

But further out, there is only sunlight over a surface—
a constant flickering, like a lit-up
airport control.

And the gulls, white as flying foam, lie beside us here
with clear balloons of air
underneath their arms.

Emptying the Desk

Lastly, in the bottom drawer, a packet.
He breaks it open. And everything there feels the same as
    ever.
This had been the first time for him.
He recalls standing in that house, in mouldy darkness.
Rain collapsed outside
like a hurled net, the trees slashing and struggling
    underneath it.
His torch-beam, about the room,
was a trapped swallow.
He had hauled back the curtains, taking hold of their heavy
    moth fur.
No sign, that night, of the distant lit suburbs.
Dead flies along the window-sill, and hung inside an open
    jar.
And rain went on rushing smoothly into the earth
through one street light
the way the gleaming sides of an express train enter a
    tunnel.
He sees again the fence-eating grass,
and, like smoke drifting, a single car
that passed in the road.
There were some hobo's dirty blankets on a mattress, to one
    corner,
trodden against the wall;
a deal table, stained and burned; two overturned aluminium
    chairs;
newspaper everywhere. There was glass underfoot
from a broken-up, heavy sideboard.

He'd moved to the next room, stepping
along a slippery path. And in there, his torch-beam fell,
    almost at once,
on someone's eyes. It leapt, like a scorched finger.
He forced it back. His heart had stabbed downward through
    his bowels.
The torch-beam, he remembers, trembled
as if it were a water-light reflected indoors.
It was someone plainly dead.
And dried blood was everywhere, the way that vandals
    smear their shit about.
She wore some scrap of underwear
and was like candle-wax. So delicate.
He has probably never, he realises, for a whole day since
    then,
quite forgotten her.
Her feet were rolled open in a clown's walk,
her arms held downwards in the way
those young girls dance.
The blood, that made crazing all over her face,
was sticking underneath her head.
She'd seemed like porcelain—a shattered figurine, with an
    expression
horrified by what had happened to itself.
All this was a long time ago.
In some of these photographs white circles are drawn;
in others, the shape of her body has been traced on the dirty
    floor.
No more since then. He's often imagined
a motel room somewhere; 3 a.m.; rain dripping in the alley;
someone propped above her,
his brain haemorrhaging its pleasure. A need going on.
All these years, that her feet have only been running in a
    few scraps of heather;
and her mouth long since has been forced open
by the root of some decorous tree.
Outside, a summer afternoon.
The secretaries are coming back from lunch, along the drive,

or are sitting on the grass together.
In a corner, between two wings of the building,
there are a few nondescript small bushes, each of them only
    leaves,
and these are stirring slightly, on the end of the light.

16 Poems

The curtains blowing
open, a sock stretched apart,
wide meadows.

Following a van, up
a winding forest road. Swallows
flit between us.

Darkness, lake-hush;
a rowboat, allowed to drift, bumps
the starlight.

As if the sun
out of boredom has doodled weeds . . .
a back yard.

This moon, the last
tilted Sauterne, in a glass
that's fire-lit.

A definition
of art deco: in black and cream
the butterfly.

Boiling water
poured from a saucepan
into a water-bottle's neck.
On the edge of your mind
the waves fall.

Wintry sunlight;
the dry, plastery legs of a woman
in tennis skirt.

Dark bedroom. Listening
to a rain-wet tree—its lovely
negligence.

Homesick for Australia,
a dream of rusty Holdens
in sunlit forests by the highway.

A cathedral interior—
these long tapers of rain lighting
candles on the twilit river.

Staved-in, the old rowboat
we had as kids
has foundered this last time
in a field of grass.

She sets the table
around a lamp. Milking-shed light
and dark mountains.

Wire coat-hangers,
misshapen, in a hotel wardrobe.
Steamy afternoon sun.

Cold swimming pool,
plastic blue. A bare tree's reflection,
its roots x-rayed.

Two magpies stepping
on the verandah. A ploughed hillside,
smoke, and cumulus.

A Day at Bellingen

I come rowing back on the mauve creek, and there's a
    daylight moon
among the shabby trees,
above the scratchy swamp oaks
and through the wrecked houses of the paperbarks;
a half moon
drifting up beside me like a jellyfish.
Now the reflected shapes are fading in the darkened rooms
    of the water.
And the water becomes, momentarily, white—magnesium
    burning.
My oars
have paused, held in their hailing
stance—
are melting;
and all the long water is a dove-grey rippled sand.
A dark bird hurries
low in a straight line silently overhead.
The navy-blue air, with faint underlighting,
has a gauze veil hung up within it, or a moist fresh smoke.
I land in the bottom of an empty paddock,
at a dark palisade
of saplings.
Among the ferns, dead leaves, fresh leaves, dry lightning-
    shaped twigs,
a cold breeze
comes up, rattling shreds all around.

A wind-blown star
is being drawn forth like a distant note.
The house I am the soul of lies,
hollow, on a ridge across the paddocks, although long
    occupied already
by the scouts of night.
I drag up the rowing boat, its rusty water slopping,
and start off, loosely in boots,
across the spongy, frog-bubbling undulations
of these coarse-bitten flats,
in a sharpened cow-dung smell.
After a day of sitting about,
spent reading and scribbling on margins
or bits of windy paper, and in remembrances,
the hours of which have passed
the way that water-drops fill at the downwards tip
of a twig,
I took the rowing boat out.
Rowed miles,
into the river, and downstream, over an ale-coloured
    brackishness—
through the societies of midges, in their visual uproar
(bronze-lit, like Caesar come to the Forum),
right out, equidistant from shore;
saw the birds swing on long trapezes across the green
    alcoves;
and followed all the notations of the tree-line
to those at dusk like flaking rust.
I came back with the slow-motion strides of a water spider
    over fluttered water.
As always, it has worked.
Now the mind is turned down, like a gas flame
in a dark kitchen,
where the wind and all the night sounds can again be heard.
It lies once more beneath the truth of the body.
All of my demanding
has become, crossing these paddocks, and watching the
    other stars appear

delicate as the first mould
on black bread, simply to take an axe and go on
up to the end of the cleared land, underneath a hooded
    eucalyptus forest,
to crack some firewood
from a weather-tightened grey log,
for a hot, deep bath, that I can draw out through the
    evening.

Landscape

After the tide's long gear-shifting gesture,
glimpsed among the bush,
climbing down toward ocean shallows'
tilting opalescence.

A washed sandbar, the yellow of a melon;
rocks' wet terracotta;
a viridescent cloud,
sponge-pitted, that is crinkled weeds—

these are somewhere underneath the sluice
of cellophane-clear,
fast-drawn-off-the-roller, billowing
water, light-glistened.

Leaning above this, out of rock, angophoras—
flesh-pink clamber
all over the dense, ink blueness of the sky.
Trees like Schiele's posturings.

And two of them clash, their shadows clamped on
a single stone—leaping for the sun
with fingertips
that basketball players try to grow.

Bringing the Cattle

All afternoon I've lain about in this illuminated country,
on one of the round hillsides, and have heard the squeak
of cropped grass, and smelt the cow smell, like a warm
convalescence, the cows close and oblivious, or with a sun-
drugged interest.

A hare stopped in the heat, and shivered, folding back
its ears—the same way as the butterfly did its wings, on
a plaited head of grass that hung above the ripe valley.

But now the farmer, who all year wears shorts and rubber
boots, and wades through the running shallows of paddock
grass, who cracks his cattle with a stick across their bony
outcrops, makes his voice float here.

And the cows jolt down with everything swinging—the
bellies, rounded as hammocks stretched full, and the four
long tits, on udders that are grooved and furry like a peach.

Their foreheads, between the big eyeballs' slow permanent
surprise, make a wide, hollow-sounding target for the
crowbar-wielding farmer when they've something broken or
a germ.

The hips, draped sharp Henry Moore shapes. And the
splayed feet are placed with mincing care, as if they've high
heels on.

Now a last cow is flouncing along the top of the slope,
its spider-web fine thread of slobber blown out long in the
final brightness of the sun.

The air is staining quickly with moisture, and the paddocks
fill with vacancy.

These corridors lain across the beaten grass are alight and chill. The river, willow-shouldered, that was silk in the distance, now at twilight is all ice panels.

And the mist that will lie kerosene-blue and thick as smoke, through the night an incubus on creeks and dams, and that will drag among the raided, fluttering cornstalks, and stick the turned earth thickly, is already starting to seep from every dark socket of the ground.

So, following the cattle, and at their pace, I am also going down.

Karl Marx

Karl Marx was playing a parlour game
with his daughters. To their question
What is the quality one should most abhor?
he wrote: Servility.

This was found—a scrap of paper
amongst the family albums and letters;
it is the most essential of all
the Complete Works.

Watching by the Harbour

There is a late Sunday over the leaf-smoke suburbs.
The sidling of a candle snuffed
sets forth
above the burred metal plate of the bay.

And that smoke quickly becomes as frail and failing
in the strength of wintry light
as Oates
walking out alone into Antarctica.

Now the sky has paled like a butcher's clean shirt.
Far beneath it, a spread seagull
idly tries
its segments of a compass inscription.

Afternoon seems light that's escaping beneath a door.
In a cooling breeze the water shrivels
the same as flesh—
It happens mostly on the surface of the mind.

The plaster-thick paint of an end wall, in that hillside,
is gold-leafed, a moment, among
makeshift eucalypts.
Cattle-tracks of clear light trodden on the water.

At this Reserve, the deep shadow of a ligamented fig,
a tilted lawn, the harbour set with sails
like restaurant tables.
Now early lights come out, smoky as lanterns.

"O time too swift, O swiftness never ceasing."—This world,
it seems, is rattling in a gypsy's
hands, that part
and reveal how the things we love have gone.

The hills shall be valleys, and the valleys will be hills.
And someone who could drag open
a bow, in youth,
has fired away their life, lost with the arrow.

Fully dark; lit by distant hordes. And along the foreshores
you see now where there is nailed
a human warmth.
Our bivouac's encircled, in mountainous night.

Diptych

1

My mother told me how one night, as would often happen,
    she'd stayed awake
in our weatherboard house, at the end of a dark, leaf-
    mulched drive,
waiting for my father, after the pubs had closed,
knowing he would have to walk
miles, "in his state",
if no one brought him home
(since, long before this, he had driven his own car off a
    mountain-side,
and, becoming legend, had rode
on the knocked-down banana palms
of a plantation, right to the foot, and someone's door,
the car reared high on a great raft of mutilated, sap-oozing
    fibre;
from which he'd climbed down, unharmed, his most soberly
    polite,
and never driven again).
This other night, my mother was reluctant to go out, and
    leave us kids asleep,

and fell asleep herself, clothed, on the unopened bed,
but leapt upright, sometime later, with the foulest taste—
glimpsed at once
he was still not there—and rushed out, gagging,
to find that, asleep, she'd bitten off the tail
of a small lizard, dragged through her lips. That bitterness (I
    used to imagine),
running onto the verandah to spit,
and standing there, spat dry, seeing across the silent, frosty
    bush
the distant lights of town had died.

And yet my mother never ceased from what philosophers
    invoke, from "extending care",
though she'd only ever read the *Women's Weekly*,
and although she could be "damned impossible" through a
    few meal-times, of course.
This care for things, I see, was her one real companion
in those years.
It was as though there were two of her,
an harassed person, and a calm, that saw what needed to be
    done, and
seemed to step through her, again.
Her care you could watch reappear like the edge of tidal
    water
in salt flats, about everything.
It was this made her drive out the neighbour's bull from our
    garden with a broom,
when she saw it trample her seedlings—
back, step by step, she forced it, through the broken fence,
it bellowing and hooking either side sharply at her all the
    way, and I
five years old on the back steps calling
"Let it have a few old bloody flowers, Mum."
No. She locked the broom handle straight-armed across its
    nose
and was pushed right back herself, quickly, across the yard.
    She
ducked behind some tomato stakes,

146

and beat it with the handle, all over that deep hollowness of
    the muzzle,
poked with the millet at its eyes,
and had her way, drove it out bellowing; while I, in torment,
stood slapping into the steps, the rail, with an ironing cord,
or suddenly rushed down there, and was quelled, also,
repelled to the bottom step, barracking. And all,
I saw, for those little flimsy leaves
she fell to at once, small as mouse prints, amongst the
    chopped-up loam.

2

Whereas, my father only seemed to care that he would
    never appear a drunkard
while ever his shoes were clean.
A drunkard he would define as someone who had forgotten
    the *mannerisms*
of a gentleman. The gentleman, after all, is only known,
only exists, through manner. He himself had the most
    perfect manners,
of a kind. I can imagine no one
with a manner more easily, and coolly, precise. With him,
manner had subsumed all of feeling. To brush and dent the
    hat
which one would doff, or to look about, over each of us, and
    then unfold a napkin
to allow the meal, in that town where probably all of the
    men
sat to eat of a hot evening without a shirt,
was his passion. After all, he was a university man
(although ungraduated), something more rare then. My
    father, I see, was hopelessly melancholic—
the position of those wary
small eyes, and thin lips, on the long-boned face
proclaimed the bitterness of every pleasure, except those of
    form.
He often drank alone

147

at the RSL club, and had been known to wear a carefully-
     considered tie
to get drunk in the sandhills, watching the sea.
When he was ill and was at home at night, I would look into
     his bedroom,
at one end of a gauzed verandah,
from around the door and a little behind him,
and see his frighteningly high-domed skull under the lamp-
     light, as he read
in a curdle of cigarette smoke.
Light shone through wire mesh onto the packed hydrangea-
     heads,
and on the great ragged mass of insects, like bees over a
     comb, that crawled tethered
and ignored right beside him. He seemed content, at these
     times,
as though he'd done all he could to himself,
and had been forced, objectively, to give up.
He liked his bland ulcer-patient food
and the big heap of library books I had brought. (My
     instructions always were:
"Nothing whingeing. Nothing by New York Jews;
nothing by women, especially the French; nothing
translated from the Russian.")
And yet, the only time I actually heard him say that he'd
     enjoyed anything
was when he spoke of the bush, once. "Up in those hills,"
he advised me, pointing around, "when the sun is coming
     out of the sea, standing amongst
that tall timber, you can feel at peace."
I was impressed. He asked me, another time, that when he
     died
I should take his ashes somewhere, and not put him with
     the locals, in the cemetery.
I went up to one of the hills he had named
years earlier, at the time of day he had spoken of, when the
     half-risen sun
was as strongly-spiked as that one
on his Infantry badge,

and I scattered him there, utterly reduced at last, amongst
    the wet, breeze-woven grass.
For all his callousness to my mother, I had long accepted
    him.
After all, he'd given, or shown me, the best advice,
and had left me alone. And I'd come by then to think that
    everyone is pathetic.
Opening his plastic, brick-sized box, that morning,
my pocket-knife slid
sideways and pierced my hand—and so I dug with that one
into his ashes, which I found were like a mauvish-grey
    marble dust,
and felt that I needn't think of anything else to say.

Aubade

The cold night that was clamped on the land
falls loose, an unwound
vise, and is lifted off.

Light rises on the spider's web,
the way a needle-drawn thread
is pulled through, to arm's length.

The room is a bush clearing,
a bale of light. A professional's grooming
these curtains, as in their youth.

And your long bright hair is like
the first paint-loaded brush stroke
that wanders before me over the white cloth.

Memories of the Coast

It used to often seem there was no one in the main street
    weekdays,
and the road, going on, dipped beneath the sea;
a wind moving along the water, as though it were among
    grass tips,
beyond tarry telegraph wires, and the shoals and flat sheen
    of the bitumen.
We kids would come up from the beach onto four o'clock
    footpath heat—
hobbling barefoot and fast between awnings,
with our seawater towels, sand-chafing floppy shorts, zinc
    cream, spiked hair;
three or four of us, and dog—counting change,
once more, by the milkbar window's bleached posters, dead
    flies.
A brick side wall there had a Bushell's sign more deeply
    blue than the sky.
On the way up, we came underneath a high paling fence,
    overhung with paspalum heads,
along a pathway of squeaking, flat-footed sand,
past some backyards—the woodpiles, cardboard boxes,
    lavatories,
long weeds, wide underwear—
and off to the other side, a black railway goods yard;
coming out on shop fronts, that always looked half-witted,
    with their sun-in-the-eyes squint.
How poignant used to seem to me the beautiful, one-
    handed lady mannequin.
She was among bolts of cloth as big as papyrus rolls seemed
    on Sunday school cards.
We went reverently indoors, at Papandreou's—
to long floorboards, dusty air, the ice-cream scoops in a jar
    of milky water,
a dried shark's jaw,
flypaper so thickly used it was like a necklace of apple-pips,

chairs stacked on tables;
to a fifty year old bristled man who came chewing from out
      the back, the woman's side of it cut short,
for a threepenny-ha'penny sale.

At that time, there were only a few fibro weekenders
      around, off among the sandhills' fluttered grass,
with watertanks on damp-rotted stands, flyscreens hung
      askew,
a rusty dog-chain stretched toward a puddle.
Behind those places, the slant, low trees seemed fused in a
      solid black clump,
coarse-leafed and sapless;
and when we came out from playing our games there, all
      through that sandy, speckled bush,
onto blue metal and dust at the level crossing,
we'd always see a few Aboriginals
going with a bottle to the sandhills, on flat pod feet.
Beyond the line, the one hotel's high verandah stood on
      insect legs, above the emollient of a pavement
that was constantly hosed, shifting dogs.
In the early fifties, most houses of town were sown loosely
      along the first few hillslopes
(under mountains that moved through every blue tone
of iris petals,
back within the land's smoulder, that reversed sea-spray).
The dusty streets had mainly weatherboards
on low stilts; no kerbs, but each place with its concrete front
      path,
and silvered steep roofing iron,
and rhubarb in the back yard.
At St John's, there'd often be a heifer browsing, Biblically,
just outdoors from the baptismal font;
and inside, someone had told me once, there was a
      fisherman laid out, all his flesh
green-bearded with dangling prawns.
These houses looked over the shops and the ply-mill smoke;
      the muscle-building

bend of the Coast railway line;
the tiles of the school; listless rugby goalposts; sandhills;
the afternoon drizzle on the ziggurats
of timber—stacks of peeled eucalyptus poles;
the Melanesian-looking spindly construction of the long
    jetty with its crane;
a few gull-molested fishing boats;
the timber boat, being slowly trodden down, before
    disappearing;
the estuary, that often held an ochre sandbank
of perfect river-pebble shape,
onto the sea, momentarily changing, and too huge to really
    look at, stretching the head apart.
All this is gone now, of course, under concrete, car-parks,
    and highways;
even the sea has been largely blocked out—
We shall sleep no more.
And I am like a salmon, that can't forget the place where it
    was born,
and only wants to return there. Nowhere
is like that any longer.

What I most often remember now, of all this time,
is just one afternoon. I had come home early from school, on
    my own, and my mother called me
to get the washing in.
Clouds were coming up like the Zulu tribes.
And it seemed such a big deal, to be helping your mother in
    that way, when she was excited—
she was flying along the clothes-line, plucking leaf and
    flower.
There was a train's whistle
from the shunting yard. I carried everything—
it was bundled into a sheet, and slung across my shoulder.
    The first raindrops,
blown, I told myself were spears
all around me, as I was jerked about, and bounced, running
    up the back yard. Some big splattered wounds,
but I made it

onto the verandah. Getting dark in there, behind the trellis,
where leaves were scraping. And she spoilt it all,
by throwing inside a floorcloth, and a ragged bathmat, and
    running out into battle again,
for the peg box—which I'd have done. She came back
    soaked, soaked all over,
in a suddenly steaming rain. No one could have survived
    it.—
I dropped that game, not to think of such a thing.

For Harriet

A pewter-coloured,
atomized steam

is left in the early, sunlit
bathroom,

and there the child has found
a cameo

of privacy. I pass
that smoke-breathing

doorway, and see how she has stepped
down

into the fields of women;
stooped

with hair-brush
to the first harvest

of her
uncertain pleasures.

153

At the Inlet

1

In the dawn an eagle leaves the forest; now the flat sea is lichened with the sun. The fish will be sparks of darkness, pouring through the water. And those thick-fingered long wings cup and undulate, loose and watery on the air.

2

Thus nature maintains itself without my concurrence; before it all my subjectivity has no standing and is dissolved. In taking it to myself, I find an incomparable satisfaction.

3

While the surrealists, who sought the Marvellous, that is hidden somewhere within us, have produced only the grotesque. How detestable, their facile sacrifice of the beauty which things have—

4

The dust on a sunlit window-pane; the life of the pores, of the hairs along the shin; the globed moisture on the upper lip; and the nipple, made of little packed, flattened globes, like a boysenberry, unripe pink. Inevitable that I should think of D., "the bird of loudest lay" . . .

5

I've opened the petals on the bud in her flesh. Branches ache around the powdered moon; contralto stars. She arches on her back; her face is soaring; her breasts seem wind-compacted. The lights of a town across the bay, like the broken streamers of our departure. And a salty snail-glitter of stars down the glass. We are lying among the strewn dominoes of the night.

6

Is this world of ours being scattered, the flying rubble from burst Paradise? So my mother taught, but I can only believe it when overlong in the cities, amongst other men.

7

Nature, in Chinese religion, is the creator of itself. It is not necessarily benign nor hostile to man, who is just a part, and must find his place within its being. The name of this teaching is sanity.

8

A ladle has been hung by an open kitchen window. Forest, ocean, sky.

9

With the natural object, an artist has all he needs to express himself. This dictum of Pound's was foreseen by Aristotle: Nothing in the mind that isn't first in the senses. Therefore, it can be said that life's fulfilment is in the contemplation of matter.

10

The true nature of the world is not different to the things we see. "One should not cling to an essence that is separate from the outside of things. When one sees mountains and rivers, he sees the Buddha-nature: when one sees the Buddha-nature, he sees the cheeks of a donkey or the mouth of a horse."

11

An early morning sea with a row of streetlights burning, a bare railway platform, and the few late stars. All that has beauty in human experience only exists this way because of death.

12

And the nothingness of death is not so vast or terrible;
it is more like something intimate. It's of my size, exactly.

13

Since the ego of an individual can be shown to be an illusion
(which we experience as estrangement and lifelessness), any
philosophy that finds an ego in the universe—God, or some
abiding Absolute—reinforcing, and rising out of, such illusion,
must itself be equally false.

14

The fibrous grasses that grow sparsely across the sandhills
flicker. If grass were measured on a scale beside water, this
would be a trickle from rusty pipes. And the broken palings
of the back fence are plaited with old bloodied strands of
wire. The fence sags full of sand, and yet is eloquent as a
mainsail, in its curving before the sea.

Mr Nelson

Their house was old grey weatherboards, on a small town
    back-street
of shale and potholes and white dust;
the verandah in lattice
from which some last off-white paint was almost gone.
It was down a slope,
on low posts that were hidden by blue hydrangeas
at the front, and had two concrete steps, and a steep, gravel-
    rashed iron roof.
The picket fence was unpainted, also,

tall paspalum
growing amongst it, where the scythe or push-mower
    couldn't reach.
I used carefully to pull a long, pale strand
of that round grass
from deep in its coarse outer sheaths, not breaking it,
    getting a very long
curved frond, and would lightly
touch my mother's arm
with the asymmetrical head, while she was talking over the
    fence there,
to get her to come along.

Almost all of the houses on this sunlight-dragged, smoke-
    idling street
were alike, except those with louvres
above their verandah sides, or a faded canvas blind.
A few newer places, in fibro,
had flat roofs, and were painted
with army surplus undercoat, pink or aquamarine.
Where some young people lived, I remember,
there'd be an old car in the front yard, its parts seemingly
    always spread on the grass,
and a wireless playing loudly from indoors.
The songs I'd hear,
my forehead leaned against the fence, while flattening an
    ant's nest with my shoe,
or trying to heap it up again,
were things like "Ghost Riders in the Sky", and "The Streets
    of Laredo",
and "Half As Much":
If you lo-ved me halfasmuch as I love you,
You wouldn't st-ay a-way halfasmuch as you do,
sung by a whiny female voice. I hated that one.

Along the top of the low, cleared hills, behind those deep
    backyards,
there was some remaining bush, and this
used to seem so dreary,

like the old cooking-splatters and fly-specklings of a kitchen
    wall.

Mrs Nelson would come out
to talk with my mother over the fence;
small and dried-up
with a voice like little bundles of twigs snapping and giving.
She was nervous-eyed as a hen,
and had a very hollow throat, inside its slack strings.
She'd had a young daughter, killed by a car
while riding a bike,
and so my mother used to always speak of Mrs Nelson as
    "that poor thing".

Standing at their front gate, making the latch click open and
    shut, gently,
careful not to be told, in mid-conversation, to get away,
or to have my hand slapped,
I could look down into their door and through the house,
    out to the bright-lit,
bleached backyard, with its long sapling clothes-line poles
that held up tea-towels, sheets and bloomers.
And I'd sometimes see Mr Nelson's shape,
his prolapsed stomach, in the blue singlet he always wore,
crossing their kitchen, at the end of the hall. Barefoot on the
    lino, he carried
a teapot and newspaper,
or half a loaf of bread on its board, or a tin of jam
with open, serrated top. Sometimes he'd come out
and offer me a Ginger Nut biscuit, if he saw me looking
    though the gate-slats,
and then he'd say, just a bit more loudly,
"Your copper's boiling."
He seemed a peculiar man,
diffident even with a child, and so polite and embarrassed
    with my mother.
He had a broad, cracked face, with what I see now
as a glaze of grief over it,

that had seemed then like a feeling of sickness, in the light,
and so I suppose I'm remembering him from shortly after
      his daughter's "accident".

One time my mother told me, after we'd left their gate and
      were hurrying on,
going to visit my grandparents around the corner,
      something else
about the Nelsons.
—I don't know what Mr Nelson's job was, although I
      remember
he once wore black sump-oil boots,
but he evidently could walk home through the cemetery,
at the end of their street, where the daughter was buried,
and he must have got off early, as Council workers do,
      because this happened
in hot afternoon sun.
(I've seen the cemetery there at such a time:
glary marble along the hill, amongst orange clay and grey,
      poor grass,
underneath a sudden cliff-face of dark bush,
with cicadas shrilling
in the heat so loud they made your head feel
it was being spun rapidly within.)
Among those dusty, bleached-out plastic flowers, and the
      jars of black water,
Mr Nelson had come on a large brown snake,
curled in the sun, on a grave-top.
He'd looked for something to kill it with, creeping off
backwards, and had only been able to grab a bit of rusty
      iron fence,
from a sunken grave, that he could work loose, that had
lumps of concrete sticking to it,
and he struck with this—
but the metal was awkwardly bent, he was hitting onto
the hill below, and the snake
heard him, so that even though he swung several times, it
      got away,

into a hole down the side of someone's grave.
The trouble was, he'd been seen
from a distance, seemingly smashing about,
by a person who had gone and told the minister, who'd
inspected, and told the police, and so on. That bit of rail
was decorated and barbed, and had scratched the head-
    stone's face
as he tried to bash close beside it. Mrs Nelson said to Mum
that for the damage he'd caused
they were being sued by someone or other, a big noise in
    town.
And they had no money,
with the funeral expenses, recently. My mother was very
    sad and annoyed
about this happening at such a time "to that poor woman".

When I was about fifteen, with a taste for Romantic poetry,
I used to wander around in the graveyard sometimes—my
    grandparents were there by then—
where I once found
a very scratched and chipped headstone. (Perhaps the case
against Mr Nelson had been lost,
or the money was used for something else.) And I could
    work out,
mainly with my fingertips,
there'd been a particularly unctuous verse, something about
God wanting the best early, for Himself,
once carved upon it.

"Following the wheel tracks . . ."

Following the wheel tracks, that had long been overgrown, he came at length to the end of the forest. And the whole sky, from all the dark horizons, was adrift with grazing stars. After a while, it seemed those stars were dangled water, and the freshness of the night was breathed from them. In the dim fields below the hillside, nothing moved. Except, far off, among some clumps of trees, which were merely slightly darker stains, a light, occasionally travelling. He wasn't sure, but perhaps the faintest sound reached him, hung in immensity, from that distant road.

Curriculum Vitae

1

Once, playing cricket, beneath a toast-dry hill,
I heard the bat crack, but watched a moment longer
a swallow, racing lightly, just above the ground. I was
    impressed by the way
the bird skimmed, fast as a cricket ball.
It was decided for me, within that instant,
where my interests lay.

And the trajectories at dusk of random moths and lone
    decisive swallow
will often still preoccupy me, until dew occludes the air.

2

I can remember there were swallows that used to sew
    together
the bars of a cattle yard.
I would be sitting in morning sunlight
on the top rail, to feel its polished surface
beneath my hands.
A silvery, weathered log that had the sheen of thistle's flax.

3

A cow was in the stocks with the calm expression of a
    Quaker;
and my father stretched his fingers,
a pianist seated on a chopping block. He bent his forehead
    to an instrument
out of Heath Robinson—
a dangling bagpipes, big as a piano,
that was played by tugging on organ stops.
The cow began to loosen its milk: its tits were disgorged,
the size and colour of small carrots;
and milk was flourished in the bucket, two skewer-thin
    daggers
sharpened on each other underhand.
Then, as the bucket filled, there would be the sound of a tap
    running
into deep suds at the end of a bath.
Finally, the calf was let in,
and this sounded like a workman building-up a big lather
    between his hands.

The concrete in those bails was shattered, but lay together
as though a platform of river stones; and water ran there
    constantly
from a hose, breaking up and bearing off
the hot lava of any cow-pats. That water was delicate and
    closely-branched—
a long weed fluttering, on such a breezy morning.

4

There were great dents of cloud-shadow on the blue-
    forested mountain;
and far off, over
the paddocks, through midday heat, the fluttering silk scarf
of a light purple range.
Our mountain was the kite, and those in the distance, its tail,
through all the heat-wavering days.

And many broken, dead trees had been left standing about,
like stone ruins: pillars that held out the remnants
of cloisters and fine stonework,
with rubble beneath them. But the air was so clear; so
    uncrowded
with any past—
arbitrary corridors, unpeopled, through the air.
Room for the mind to travel on and on.
I used to have to stop, often, to stand there, in that immense
    amphitheatre
of silence and light.

5

I remember watching our three or four geese let loose and
    rushing,
with their heads beating sideways like metronomes,
towards a dam where the mountain-top hung;
and when they entered the water, the mountain's image
    came apart
suddenly, the way a cabbage falls into coleslaw.
Everything was changed, as easily as that.

6

Since then, I have been, for instance, in Petticoat Lane—
    pushing by
through narrow, stacked alleys,
among the tons of rotting garbage for sale,

and have seen the really poor.
Those people seemed just dangling paper dolls, threaded
    onto
a genetic string—
the characters of poverty, starch, lack of sun,
and stunted, hopeless spirit everywhere. Their crossed eyes,
    warts,
twisted faces, snaggle teeth,
drunkenness were Dickens still, in '70 something,
again in '82.—People in greasy rags, on crutches, weeding
    wet butts
from the gutters;
spiky-haired, furtive, foul-muttering.
The women were shaped like slapped-together piles of clay.
    They scrabbled
amongst junk, viciously,
yelling to each other, and oblivious . . .

What is such an evil, but the continuing effect
of capital's Stalinism?
Enclosure, as John Clare has said, lets not a thing remain.

And then, an hour later, in the West End I found
how much worse I thought an askance,
meringue-coloured, prissy-lipped upperclass face—so sleek
in its obliviousness.
People go rotten with culture, also.

7

Another time, in Washington, when my girlfriend had gone
to see someone,
and while I was sitting at an upstairs window, I watched the
    bald man
who lived next door, after he'd argued once more
with his wife, come out to stand alone
in their backyard—round as a pebble, in his singlet,
but nowhere near so hard.

He was standing with chin sunk
holding the garden hose—a narrowed stream
he felt around with
closely, like a blind man's cane.
It disturbed me to see him like that—but then, as I started
    to consider myself,
I saw that I was walking
in those silver paddocks, again,
which as a kid I'd known.

8

Or, travelling alone in Europe once, and staying in a
    provincial city,
indolent and homesick of an afternoon,
I turned, as ever, to the museum.
In such a mood, however, the masterpiece will often no
    longer serve:
it seems too strenuous and too elevated;
it belongs in a world too far beyond one's own.
From experience, one has learned at these times to follow
    that arrow, *Ecole francaise*
XIXe siècle. There, on an attic floor,
unnoticed by the attendant, a newspaper crumpled
over his boots, or along the deserted outer corridors,
beneath tall windows, in the light from which
many of them are cancelled,
hang one's faithful mediocrities—in sympathy with whom
one had thought to be borne through until dinnertime.
Armand Guillaumin, Léon Cogniet, Jules Dupré, Félix Ziem:
no artistic claims can be made for these. Their sluggish or
    bituminous pigment,
greasy sheen, and craquelure,
their failures, so complex and sad, have earned them
"an undisturbed repose".
And yet, even these harmless,
unassuming, and forgotten, as I glanced among them, on
    this occasion,

were forgotten
by their one idle, arbitrary re-creator,
and the landscapes that came far more vividly before my
    eyes
were all memories.

9

Into my mind there has always come, when travelling,
images of the twisted Hawkesbury bush
crackling in the heat, and scattering its bark and twigs
    about,
white sunlight flicked
thickly on the frothy surges
and troughs of its greenery; and within those forests,
great pools of deep fern, afloat
beneath a sandstone rock-lip; and of the Platonic blueness
of the sky; and recollections of Coledale and Thirroul
on their clifftops, where sea-spray
blows among the pines and eucalypts; and, most of all, of
    those forests,
cool, light-flouncing, with white female limbs,
and the yeasted green pastures,
where my mind first opened, like a bubble from a glass-
    blower's tube,
and shone, reflecting
things as they are—
there, where I have felt, anxiously, I would find them
a while longer,
after passing Kempsey, once more, on the mail train of an
    early morning.

PIANO

Black Landscape

All of the high country, that year, had been burned out
with the headline blackness of war.
Soon afterwards we came travelling through the place,
along a ridge's blade-edge by car.

The tree-forms then were the crudest of hieroglyphs—
a crushed charcoal scrawl;
petrified in their extreme gestures, about those hills
steep as a landslide sprawl.

Rain-storms had just been there; in overcast light
boulders exuding shine.
And the clinkered valleys were backed with high, wet cliffs.
An immense open-cut coal mine.

We were creeping through winds that pounded on the car;
twanged it; made it a cripple;
that seemed to compress its shape. But stopped to
        photograph;
the car braced like a mule.

Climbed down, into stillness and deadness. The clay slopes'
squirming runnels, closely traced,
left earth hung between horizontal strata—a Hindu facade,
now almost effaced.

A crow was blown away, with a shout; I thought of having
        to eat
such dry fibre. Keats didn't know
all about those syllables, "forlorn", who'd never heard
a sound like the bushfire's crow.

Everywhere, great ruptured webs, the shining charcoal
        bushes.
Twigs traced and smudged us black.

I saw ahead, in profile, how a cliff-face was built of shale:
the silverfishes' newspaper stack.

Smell of wet ashes, and trickling of water. We found
headless trees breaking there
into fine leaves, again: the boles were stockinged with them
as with flame. A tremulous mohair.

In red and green of an apple. So: fire, air, water, earth;
each contending with another;
shifting of energies, as animals shove in their sleep. And life,
too, where things are sore.

I took from beneath a stone the cicada: six-legged tottering;
three clear jewels on its brow;
an orange samurai mask. Those beautiful gauze wings
segmented with a gum tree bough.

Between such branches, if you tilt your hand, you can make
a light, pale blue and frail
as after sunset. I told a girl once, in Ireland, of cicadas;
she said, "We only ever had a snail."

Configuration

Smoke is stirring its haunches slowly
at the dark end of the platform—
the nebulae.

The tall heads of weeds are frail
in a sparse lamp-light
over gravel.

In the waiting room, a viscous shine
on plank walls' and benches'
sluggish green.

We are waiting outside, at the edge
of the varnished light;
our breaths merge.

Space and night, and the windy rush
of the train, far off
in the bush.

The stars are a salt-freighted wind
where the Department's red lights
are pinned.

Matins

The bricks drawn off the brick stack,
two together, scrape on their brick dust
and clink and chime, glassily and brittle,
as they're stacked afresh, into his barrow
by the bricklayer's mate, who wears
large gloves, that are mauve and stiff as
old rabbit hides. The bricklayer's mud
lies stirred and ready on its boards,
with the same colour, and looseness,
and pendulous weight, as an elephant's
haunch. The off-sider's boots scuff
the smears of mortar across the pavement,
grind on pebbles, resound hollowly in the
slack board ramp, on which they tramp,
making a single loose bass string's sound—
desultorily and thickly-fingered struck.

Orange-red leaves will be dripping from
the pavement trees, under a grey sky,
about the kerb: whimsical and idle like
an Ophelia's petals, and yet serious, too.
The trees' sift is counterpoint to all that
stomping, or the shearing, gravel-slicing
sound of the spatula, that knocks and
is drawn again, through its grating slide.
All the time, sparrows hop like hot fat,
underneath a dim tree, making their sharp
decibels of sound, over and over, or stop
to puff and rewind the simple mechanism
of excess. And now, a long underbelly sound
of a tarpaulin, dragged upon to slide.
And I hear the steady, firm high heels of
what must be a young woman passing by,
and this knocking is not hollow, the way
workmen's noise is, nor like the traffic,
harried, and how it builds a calf and thigh,
and buttocks, and those rower's cables,
the spinal muscles, that are shaped by light,
and sheened, and finally has called me up
out of the deep blankets, to the day.

A Port of Europe

Like a bandage in a gorse bush, water gleams
on the dark-clouded moor,
and far off, in the other direction, along the top of the world,
lies a slat of metal ocean, under
frail moonlight.
The moon is resonant on the sea as though a gong-face had
    been flicked
with a fingernail.

And one dark, cowled farmhouse, with chalky jowls, drowses
stiffly here, in a hallway for the winds—
it is the nun who keeps a door.
Westward from Flensburg, on these low marshlands
of saturated green,
air capers wildly
as children of the poltergeist,
vaulting far over the metronome monotony of windmills, and the few small startled horses
with wind-hacked manes.
The shoreline and fields are mere sediment of the coagulating sky.
The ocean shifts as though weight-lifted oil,
and under old jetties undulates
lubriciously as crazed inmates on the poles.
Black outer waters of ocean jostle
and bound, a herd of migrant tusks, that mills and advances again,
and fills one with dread, imagining
the blankly inhuman nature
of a primal force.
While along this shoreline, on sandhills, is a wild adulatory dance:
the hose-loose waverings of coarse grass.
A small town flies the moon with its flags,
among casques of verdigris. The landscape stares in, down the streets,
and carries within its cloak
the cock of mockery.
Spires and clock-chimes, and amongst them a few sails
cupped and pulsing softly, like pale jelly-fish;
and long water-logged barges
that burrow in a deep grey or moss-black estuarine water.
Over the acres of sea-front, dieseline
and urinous salt. Here, the parlours of casseroles and geraniums,
of alcohol, onion-rings, pipe smoke,
and old fish-nets dried as roots. A patina of human grease

is on every stone and sill. And these scratched, pewter-
      coloured faces—
are these the heads of tragic clowns
or a potato harvest?
The clouds at sunset were vast, lurid fungi:
damp purples, yellows, and vermilion. One sail
like a drifting spore—
the long-tailed seed of a pine cone, that had burst in a
      distant fire—
was wavering there,
towards what seemed the mountainous country of the sky,
but it will have fallen again
upon this shore.

Very Early

Birds are drifting, bubbles on the eyesight, in a frangipani
      sunrise.
Waves nod as a rocking horse would,
if it were one that left standing before long windows could
stir with the air. Now on the bay lies
the diamond flotilla. And right the length of the harbour
a light stretches: one duellist, and the other.

The weavings of an immediate Penelope; and then, a vast
      trunk of light
speckled about with a leaf-shimmer
of light-points. On many a verandah
you see where the summer mist of the mosquito net
is still abroad. The hypotenuse at ease.
Curlicues on a dog's back are being planed by a breeze.

The dog, tongue loose as a pocket hanging out,
is leaving the reserve (these roman candles of green,

173

the lawns pebbly with dew, and moored yachts with their
    bathroom sheen);
it blows away into the open barn door of a street—
dimly and complacent, follows some hunch.
A small, dark bird in there shifts like a sparkle on a branch.

Here at the park, a turbaned snail, the potentate of the dew,
majestically moves. Gum leaves are eyebrows being drawn
on light. A spider hangs in the midst of dawn.
The pine trees, at a distance, seem water-stains down a
    plastery blue.
If no-one saw all this, its existence would go on just as well.
And what is really here no words can tell.

Rainy Windows

Wildly flourished, little pods of water;
and these long runnels, drawn among them, for the stalks—
it is a frieze of shivery grass.

A puffed diffidence, of floaty, pattered weeds.
Or a carbonated glass, in which the apothegmatic bubbles
are pressured down.

Through gauzy water, gate-posts,
tiles, chimneys, black tentacles, and the sudden leaf-twitches
of birds leaping, without birds.

The pavement twitches. Out there,
the land of "the Anthropophagi, and (of those) whose heads
    do grow
beneath their shoulders."

Across my room, a window's lizard skin,
silverish-grey. Going over, the world is in all the jumbled
colours, and fogginess, of a wok.

One keeps returning: to what's also the smudge
on chilled white grapes. Within it, the light of a chardonnay.
Approached, a fluttery veil—frail

and dotty. A Zelda Fitzgerald, though one
calmer now. This tender collector of sodden lengths of
      string.
Along the road, soda fuzziness

as lights appear in late afternoon.
It has all become a watercolourist's first essay, washed off
beneath the tap. A miscegenated grey.

In such weather, only largeness matters,
bases endure. The watcher's allowed an intimation of release
in the detachment of this flickery change.

I always find with such weather an utter
accord. As when, grown still, one lies sidelong to consider
the perspiring face of one's love.

Byron Bay: Winter

      Barely contained by the eyesight,
      the beach makes one great arc—
      blue ranges, overlapping, behind it;
      each of them is a tide-mark.

About me, the swamp-oaks' foliage
streams: hatching by Cézanne.
Off in the scrub, a guard's carriage
following the vats of a train.

A creek spoils the hem of the sea,
spread on the beach in flutes;
it had that redness in black tea,
and the smell of sodden roots.

Behind me, a purple cloud swells,
the colour of old claret stain.
The sunlit town, midden of shells;
its lighthouse is a tiny pawn.

I'm walking on the beach alone;
the sea's grey feathers flurry,
showing emerald. Sandpipers blown:
mice among birds, in their scurry.

And the sun on my shoulders brings,
because of its perfect warmth,
the feeling that I wear great wings
while stepping along the earth.

A Garden Shed

From ten to thirteen I was often sent
for a month or even more at a time
to my grandmother's in a distant town
after grandfather died—it was thought
I should go, though she hardly spoke.

I read by the stove; she would pause
in sewing, sometimes, and you'd see
she was out billowing about, or
crouching beside doors along the night,
pushing at some. I kept a watch;

but after school I used to wander
in the scrub behind that big-verandahed,
shabby, dislocated bungalow, beyond
her call and the other straggling houses
at the town's edge; and I saw how

once in the country the train began
wildly careering, with its horn
braying out, again and again.
When I arrived first, rain appeared:
long slashes on a carriage window

that broke up those trajectories,
so the heavy glass it seemed was chipped
at, but slowly—too slowly for escape.
I remember the clattering of a tocsin,
the railway crossing that we burst

right through—a clown and hoop;
and I was driven on, landed, lips stretched,
on my feet. It must have been
the ache at her house was the boredom,
since it was never really so good

being at home. But the mountains between
above small-town, dairy farm smoke
were a kingfisher blue, and their glint,
coming from night, was sad like a sail
that passes by. Strange you don't complain

at that age. I had the inarticulate
endurance children have, or some have.

Grandma died of her strokes, completely mad.
I'd only liked there when allowed a key
to grandfather's shed. "Just so's to look."

At the end of the long, rubbishy yard,
past lumber on trestles, the chicken run
of oil-black earth and wire netting,
the tatty eucalypts with their clothes line,
all in a high stockade of palings,

I let myself in. There, I'd rediscover
each chisel, peculiar saws, the claw
and ballpein hammers, his screwdrivers,
brace-and-bits, punches, spanners, and
a regal, African paint brush array

stood on shakily-done shadowboards—
things spiky, knobbed, sharp or frayed
like those raced among, beyond the fence,
out in the heath. I'd handle these,
but it would have been a sacrilege for me

to think them useable. (It was there
I was betrayed, my family would say.)
All of that was carefully hung,
sharp and oiled, in the gloom again,
with glints—strange, like creatures in

(were it possible) a deep-sea aquarium.
And I found beneath the workbench
sawdust still adrift in a spider's web.
There was an old sofa, brown, bleached
as though a rose petal in a book;

and stacks of bevelled, collected timber
slung overhead—how curious those
differing lengths: each had a meaning,
I felt, like poetry-shapes to be read
some day in our maroon leather Milton.

Grimy light in there made it look
always a rainy afternoon. In the quiet
I could hear the neighbour's hens creak
just outside, or washing flap,
or a car somewhere, changing gear.

And I've always wanted to live again
at the level where one lived when
looking at, or listening to, those things:
in the immense presence of that wordless
questioning. I seemed to be lying alone

out on a hillslope, until I could hear
coming through things cast-up about there
a far roaring, of their endless sea.
In the secret noise of such turmoil
and spray, I was somehow looking back—

or being looked through, about to be lost—
to my grandfather and I, who were only
bubbles of a moment, amid this whirling
away. I first recognized the frankness
of nature's appropriations there:

that it's all effectiveness, inter-response;
all mutuality and possibilities;
just things happening among themselves.
Things creating each other. And we
are only the expressions of circumstance,

of its tensions. Nothing belongs to any
separate thing. It was there I began
to understand: the less we think we are
the more we bear; and someone who sees
he is nothing, lightly will bear it all.

Harbour Dusk

She and I had come wandering there through an empty
    park,
and we laid our hands on a stone parapet's
fading life. Before us, across the oily, aubergine dark
of the harbour, we could make out yachts—

beneath an overcast sky, that was mauve underlit,
against a far shore of dark, crumbling bush.
Part of the city, to our left, was fruit shop bright.
After the summer day, a huge, moist hush.

The yachts were far across their empty fields of water.
One, at times, was gently rested like a quill.
They seemed to whisper, slipping amongst each other;
always hovering, as though resolve were ill.

Away off, through the strung Bridge, a sky of mulberry
and orange chiffon. Mauve-grey, each cloven sail—
like nursing sisters, in a deep corridor: some melancholy;
or nuns, going to an evening confessional.

Eight Poems after Kusadao

two
things

that have
no

memories

fresh

fallen
snow

a

leaping

squirrel

—

at
dawn

three or
four

often

to say
they're

wronged

—

cutting
at

the
cabbage

heart

and
a rooster

calls
far

off

in
huge

desolation

—

my
wife

two
nights

gone
for

two
nights

the
galaxy

—

a
plum

bloom
trodden

down
shows

us
this

earth

—

late
night

apples
lamp-

lit
stall

and
Orion

in glory

—

zazen
in

temple
cold

so
harsh
my

eyes
trickle

hopeless

longing

—

autumn

I
hear

cicadas
grow

fainter

with
no

resistance

Nakamura Kusadao, haiku poet, 1901–1984.
Translated with Professor Shigeo Kitagawa, Tokyo, 1985

Plurality
To Philip Hammial, the traveller from an antique land

Our flat was in a building that backed on the golf course,
and it shone with the bay. In this street
hosanna of Mediterranean palms, and Moreton Bay fig trees
pressing large fingers to the light.
Here we lived day after day.

A concrete esplanade, planted with old metal lamp-posts,
shaped the waterfront. The bay's wobble
when the tide was running in
was like the filled reboundings of a spirit level.
Or the water grey and heavy as a punt.

184

This also had its beauty. If a tug or trawler came
from under leaves, on such a day,
the bow-wave was luminously white. And gangly yachts,
subtly restless, as though they were a schoolgirls' assembly,
waited—their gowns, umbrellas rolled tight.

Out in the harbour, along the moored steamers' high black
        sides,
drifting up and down, dropping like shuttles
down a spindle, levered up again—for their tensile
wide-orbiting dance—were gulls.
The dreaming efficiency of machine parts, in the distance.

From our windows late, with lights out, the water
        shimmering
as if leaves on a tree,
the way it was lifted in the moonlight. And further on,
        toward
the moon, the harbour so gauze-like it could be
a desert—untrodden, silvery-dewed.

This was, for me, the tranquil early Eighties; I was not yet
        forty.
I've mostly lived near the sea;
part of my boyhood was remote, in the face of empty water.
I think at the end we live a similar way.
In those days, it was on a headland, yellow and dusty.

The tall sea could seem, at once, a wall and its isolate
forbidden garden. (O fertile, impossible sea.)
The earth there, with a scumbling of tight grass, was in the
        summer
zwieback. A few weatherboard houses, dry
as folds of a lizard's throat, before the jangled light.

Washing waved to nothing. Our side wall transformed
in late afternoon, like a filled sponge. For play, as a kid,

I'd a myriad small antheaps—their energy of boiling
      saucepans.
The clouds often like a motorcycle skid.
Beyond the stale mustard-colour of land, a ship went
      traipsing.

Quartz gravel, dandelions, rusty tin, the blown
dirt road, slant telephone poles, a reservoir . . .
Then, below our flat, someone swaying on a moisturized
      golf-course
beside the bay, posed like a figurine for us to admire.
I don't forget the real nature of the ocean.

If you live with that, and little else, it will come to seem a
      dream
that is fed with dreams. It deals, then keeps on and on
to regain. It's both good and evil
and will not resolve itself where you draw a line.
Long fumbling to describe it, I heard of the sky burial.

In Tibet, when someone ordinary dies, because the earth is
      sacred,
and there's such scarcity of wood,
they're laid on a large rock outside town, where an
      undertaker,
with two knives, goes to work—the body is dissected;
the skin flayed, all joints severed.

Male relatives watch from a short distance those gesturing
      tools
of a little squatting monkey, whom no-one
but outcasts will speak to, whom no doctor will treat,
his white robes growing silently spoiled. He has slit the
      body open
and piles the organs like jewels.

Briskly scores and dices flesh; takes a small sledge-hammer
to the bones, pounding each one;

he makes of the whole body, within three-quarters of an
	hour,
a neat wet pile. No pictures of this can be taken.
Into bones and flesh stirs some barley-meal.

Finally stands back, and holding wide his hands, stiff as
	prods,
those two weird flowers, he sings,
ululates, to the eroded escarpments around, the one
	extraordinary
word, of Tibetan knife-carved lettering, that brings
thumping about him an avalanche of big, loose clods—

The vultures amble over each other's backs, and slap
monstrous gloves. Saved for the leader of the flock,
now thrown him, the liver. Trampling of waves. And these
	great wings
glisten and stream. In minutes, not a sliver on the rock.
Their flight: graceful and horrible. It cancels out.

There is nowhere valuation. Everything, equally, is desire to
	live.
It is a oneness, always plural.
Yet, if someone crosses the stale ditch about themselves,
or the yachts on blueness incarnate a breeze, or a face is
	beautiful,
how this ocean's endless hunger will seem worthwhile.

Cows in Massachusetts

The cows have left the barns, and wearing their leaf-shadow
they're all through an early spring's

treeless yet filtered air;
and they moo as they barely move about, with horns low

in the grass, that is silvery and lacquered
and has its tips curled downward, too.

Across the grass comes a breeze, and so these friesians
seem to stand amid a pebbly ford;

grass so moist it smarts the air
when tugged upon, like fingers drawn down shiny glass.

The air in spring here is yellow
as cider, or cider apples—that crabbed fruit

propped on wet sticks; and one thinks of the yellow
of damp straw in barns,

like a hairdresser's combed snippings
amongst the dung;

and of the mellow colour of a turtle's stone
breast, tapped upon; the horn of a farmer's thumb

and dry palm; the scraped-out cold chicken fat;
grass ribbons in a book;

and in these woods, puffed onto mud, the curry powder
of a scuffed fungus

among the staircase roots . . . But this was about the illusion
of God's own country seeming to be,

for a passing
few minutes, where they have claimed. And about

Jasper Johns, whom someone said that one could meet
in New York,

or Andy Warhol—"I can fix it for you."
But I left there

and went on, and saw the cows pass,
who know what they like, and did not think Alas.

Walking Around at Night

The rising moon appears,
softly focused as a movie queen,
in a close frame
through the kitchen fly-screen.

I stroll outside, and down the path,
leaving the radio;
the moon is buxom
above the smoky, besom willow.

It's just the old fumy paraffin lamp
of a moon, that I prefer.
The hammer blows of barking,
a car clearing its chest, somewhere,

the slam of a tinny garage door
on concrete, and the voices
going inside, that could be either quarrelsome
or boisterous.

Iron filings are magnetized in place
about lamps, for the night;
the empty pavements' stretched rigidities
submit to that light.

A torn white paper edging
of water in a gutter.
The poplars and bushes, that wait for me to pass,
are dressed in purdah.

This dim-lit town backs
into black gullies, from the milkbar freeway:
a few novas burn
in a shapeless, dusty galaxy.

Cars and pick-up trucks pulled on the grass
under porch-shine
have a cold, metallic baldness
dusted with marzipan.

The white-painted boards of one house
wear a net veil
of leaf-shadows. These lawns, side lit,
are wheatgrass: succulent, shapely, and frail.

The parking lot is bare tonight
within a cold, immense
chain-wire, on which I hang—the shadows of some pebbles
loom like a chess defence.

A single tree on the lawn beside here,
in "subdued light", is still:
dressed up like a woman, alone in the corridor
of a convention hotel;

a skinny tree, in knee-length fashion, and
leg-aligning, high-heel pose.
Now, a little nervous, and preening—already tottery.
Another one of those.

This way, just out of town, is a tall hillshape,
a dark perfect dune,
unravelling irregularly as coarse cloth
its outline, under the moon.

A set of headlights is coming beneath it
beside corn, in colder air
from the river. I turn into the paddocks,
toward a steamy, lit fun-fair,

that's been segregated by the wind tonight
at the racecourse. I only get so near.
The music, heavy-handed makeup,
and those lights are overflowing like beer.

The rides: spun poker machines, big-jointed lumberings.
Glazed with a luminous breath,
there's a long headland of forest behind
the sad necklace of milk teeth.

Across the paddocks, backyards—
above the fences, lounge room lights burn;
in the frosty night, thick like thistle fur,
a few porch lights are on.

I keep walking, and see how a cow and the moon
are each a term
in some kind of sequence. I shoo
a cow up, for a place to lie that's warm,

under a lichen-smoke and bird's egg sky.
Adrift on the windmill night.
It gets chill. Going on, toward a razor-strop highway—
that sound, those streaks of light.

They are suddenly lifted away at the curve
and gone—each a stroke;
and there's an occasional heavy flat backward
stropping, which is a truck.

Waiting to cross (a short-cut back), I stand off
in the weeds. At every car
these are strung with glutinous, distended drops.
The moon's blue as an old scar.

Prunus Nigra

The plum tree with popcorn blossom
is pink upon the frost,
or it's embossed on the dusty blueness
of the lower sky, toward dusk.

A magpie, ragged witch-doctor,
long-jumps to the clothes-line pole;
behind it, the plum tree bursts
like a wave at sunset.

How terrible it would be
if this plum bloomed near the palings
and one saw it with the memories
of some other life.

Fire Sermon

The lissome bay is silvered slightly, in its supine lightness;
a stocking-textured water
takes the morning's cerise.

But soon, between the headlands, sea and sky are solid
     blues
that have closed, almost
seamlessly, like stone.

And yachts have come out to climb on the sea's face, slow
and wavering—the way
that cabbagemoths walk.

These foreshores are deeply tented in eucalyptus saplings
and tea-trees, leaned
on the engorged light.

Here cicadas' sizzling, strapped toffee strings of sound,
filmy and flashing, fuse
into sheets, all around.

Now the rhythmical light-points shoal the water thickly
as this shift to shovelled
gravel in cicadas' song.

Simmered eucalyptus oil vaporously uncoils, accompanying
angophoras, the dancing
Indras of rosy stone.

Dilated summer. It seems you can see into the Flame, while
light-cells teem, cicadas thrum—
to its naked sensuous events.

On the far shore, house-faces hang, a white muslin among
bush humble as rubble
in the blue Empire.

193

I've left everything behind, for an endpaper shore; to lie
under membranous layers, where
lights vault, coagulate, rebound—

To see one ignite another, billowing, and genealogies
        decline;
to watch here day's ardour
that turns water into wine.

Other People

There are rain-pebbles, late,
across black windows, streetlight on them;
they hang like conglomerate
in the cement wall of a mausoleum,

which is the darkness. Or are fused
as if a lever were thrown
when cars pass. Clear dark is bruised
where a figure sits. The telephone

keeps on. Headlights splash as though
trying to wash from the wall
a realization. One that won't let go
for anyone who'd call.

—

A public phone and pine trees on
the edge of the paddocks. You see a man
cross an oily concrete apron
to the shop's bowser. An old beer can

in here, a cigarette's long ash
on the ledge. The directory says, "My fault",
underscored. "Come on Babe." Your cash
dangles. Echo-sounds a black vault.

The cow's rump is a rowboat that takes
a wave-crest. Gritty miniatures.
A camphor laurel's lime and silver flakes.
A cloud like steam, claws over claws.

17 Poems from the Japanese

Even now, I never linger
by this valley stream,
in case my shadow
flows back into the world.
                    Dōgen

Ah, how many dewdrops are falling
from the stems of grass,
now that the autumn winds have come
to the fields of Miyagino?
                    —Saigyo

Sorcerer, who flies through heaven,
find for me the one
who has never yet appeared,
not even in my dreams.
                    —Murasaki

In the shade of a willow
by the road

the clear water is running.
I meant to pause here
only a moment.
                    —Saigyo

Water drips from moss
among the mountain stones,
and I am rendered clear.
                    —Ryokan

The days that have gone by
leave one sad,
and yet they were all of them
only a dream.
                    —Former Emperor Hanazono

I sit and look back on
days that have gone.
Did I dream them all,
am I dreaming now?
Listening to winter rain.
                    —Ryokan

It is late at night
but I can't hear the waterfall.
Perhaps there is snow falling
on the mountain-top.
                    —Ryokan

A light snowfall
and within that
a billion worlds arise
and within that
a light snowfall.
                    —Ryokan

Haze rises
at the end of a spring day
that I have spent with children
bouncing ball.
>—Ryokan

As the sunset ends
and the mountains are hidden,
further off
other mountains appear.
>—Kyoguku Tamekame

In my home town
the cherries are in bloom
and spring is passing by
the same as ever.
>—Dōgen

Early summer rain
has left in the roadway
a hall of light.
>—Basho

Ah, look!
The mushroom-gatherers missed
five dewdrops.
>—Buson

A camellia fell;
the monk smiled
going by.
>—Hori Bakusui

Clear autumn day;
my wife doesn't even notice
we pass each other.
>—Nishigaki Shu

The crows' calling
ends.
Twilight snow.

—Aro Usuda

Translated with Kazuaki Tanahashi; Zen Centre, San Francisco, 1982

The Shark

There are tons of the sea's loose flesh above, made to jostle
and shimmy,
an immense, shadow-tainted
clear jelly;

it shoulders and displaces itself
about itself, on the peaked and flaked plain,
harried like migrant reindeer,
lava-bright or wind-torn.

The diver goes on steadily sinking from there, spread on
       shadow
as to drown;
weighted, he feels ducked and
pole-pressured down.

Only his breath seems to panic, and he turns to watch it
       pass,
wobbling and clinking upward
into light;
a stairwell the mind climbs and breaks like glass.

The long sunlight sways here
in columns, as though a bundle of lift cables.
With its withered Red Indian head
a turtle's

struggling up steeply
on stumpy wings—an ennui, bound in horn,
a broken beak.
Bevies of fish are making little mouths to squeak

like society girls, in their spotted or banded
wafting chiffon,
and with impenetrable dead eyes. The jelly fish,
a huge heap of frog spawn.

Something stares sideways
that's a worn-down Caligula profile—its teeth like a fender.
And as a spinning hoop
when it is coming to rest surrounds a

centre, with touches of all parts of the rim,
so in leather skirt a rat-tailed
manta ray, flapping,
is hung in the grit it's flailed.

The shark comes drifting with silent engine
through water thick as smoke,
a space craft that is called on by a distant gravity
out of the murk;

but it can loosely swathe
its limber grey fuselage.
It moves with all the potential and ease of someone
turning out of a garage.

The long body wavers beautifully
and easily
as a train at dusk
through the curves on the floor of a valley.

The gills, for all their frightful deepness,
are each neat
as a Japanese slit;
the head's simply rounded-off and incorporate

like the nose of a surfboard—it is not the authority
for anything within;
the head, amid jungle light, seems less important
than its fin.

It has the senile, yellow, ill-wishing look
of a hillbilly grandma's
uncomprehending eyes, and what seems her mouth
in its Greek mask melancholy or tooth-stump uncouth—

but a foolish guffaw
and that vacuousness is filled with doubled barbed wire
or, closer,
a wreath with each leaf a razor.

The mouth is a picketing of backward serrations;
the skin, sliding ground glass.
The diver waits with his single fang poised, for the tonnage
of its flick-pass—

imagining the voluptuous greedy wriggle
of its packed dog's body
and himself clamped too overwhelmingly, too rigid,
for struggle.

This energy, this pure appetite, that's below
and before the mind, this
is the thriving pathology

which is life; here elegant, as though wriggled from a
      thesis.

Weakened and divided in us, this still has to be allowed for,
it is basic;
in me it has a voice,
each has a shark.

And what shall we do with this?
All things are unstable and flowing, as if the modes of one
      thing:
is it possible this could modify?
It would have to be shaped by knowing.

Only through understanding,
by staying watchful and still:
the effort to change is, as with art, love, religion, a
      deviousness
of the shark-like will.

Morality we learned,
through being outdone in immorality. Ultimately, from
      Zeus.
By wanting some time
for something other than ourself. Morality is a truce.

It arises from whence
so much evil sets forth—out of boredom. But is knowledge
and strength. It's to face our nature, without wanting to
      disclaim;
to call that by its name.

To Philip Hodgins

I sit in an empty restaurant at a table with a view
through plate glass, onto tree-tops grown dark.
The sky is a new carbon paper's deep, remote blue;
the lamps, skimmed ocean moonlight, in the park.

Foliage near those lamps looks chipped as woodcuts.
And buildings the shape of cabinets, beyond there,
are left open on digital batons—the neon lights,
arrayed with all their warmth of a questionnaire.

Midway, and dark mauve, the stone of the Cenotaph,
in art deco style; with soldiers that are Shades
along its highest ledges, led to by every path,
sat hunched in greatcoats, helmeted. This pervades

the restaurant's counterpart. Tonight, my cloth's
whiteness, glasses, silver are the projection
before it. And the napkins make tall, grave yachts
outside, beneath strange planets' conjunction.

A light is being proffered, rococo, unfunctional,
to the nearest stone conscript, who might seem,
beyond an insubstantial, glittering, decorous table,
someone who's brittle as salt, in a waiting room.

That mausoleum has the presence of Böcklin's "Isle
of the Dead". Yet, leaves blow apart; people walk
unperturbed there, within a sea so dark and mobile;
and Philip arrives with books and poems and we talk.

Piano

afternoon

promenade

late
afternoon

closing
a wood gate

paling
yards

promenade

wing
collars

seagulls

a lighthouse

the parasol
handle

promenade

spray
drifts

pollen

it clings

in muslin
watched

by
a young man

promenade

a lighter
as slow

on the

difficult
sea

spray
drifts

the low
sun

soft

and wide

is
a web

something
that matters

almost
said

long
promenades

what was
crueller

the gulls'
cry

girls'
chatter?

sea-
spray

pollen

promenades

of vanity
vanity

vanity

that
still

bemuse

the
afternoons

of an
old man

Description of a Walk

In the shape of long sand-dunes, but apple green,
the pastures that I'd crossed. A quivering rain
hung above them. One currawong somewhere, warbling
happily as a hose within a drain.

The forest was cumulus on stilts, from afar;
everywhere within it, leaf-splatterings and spar;
the leaves, paint clots, or a fringe of trickling.
Angry as a burned insect, a distant car.

The forest closed. I climbed amongst sandstone—
great gouts of lava, petrified as iron;
puffed like fungi, or with a broken iceberg's edge;
all of a rusty red or burnt orange tone.

About the plinths and mantels was an artful
pebble-scatter; on its pedestal, an eccentric bowl.
Rose-coloured sandstone syncopated salt.
Blowing rain was being emptied by the bushel.

Uphill, warped arcades of bush, rack on rack;
reiterative as cuneiforms. Bacon redness of bark,
or smooth wet trunks of caterpillar green,
and some with a close dog's fur, greyish black.

Other colours: Brazil nut kernel, an unfired pot
In the wet, tart as bush smoke, a sweet rot.
The air rain-threaded, as though with insect sounds.
My heart flapped like a lizard's, by the top.

Underneath a clay bank, an old grey gutter,
now filled—rare smoked glass. A claw of water
flexed nearby, on rock ledges, and over roots—
its wide-toothed, vibrating cane-rake clatter.

Sprigged trees, and vista of Pre-Raphaelite shine:
beneath gentian hills, a billiard table green;
ploughed land, pumpernickel; the road, a fracture;
the shapes of coral in a dark tree-line.

Rain shaded to silence. To cicadas' shekel
sound.—Emptied from a bucket, a pile of shell
poured with the numerous headlong pour of sand
onto other shells. A dry calcite rattle.

And this merely the start—warming of an engine.
Each opens a row of gills; if you find one
you see almost through the body. Their joined hums'
tremendous power, an electricity substation.

I walked on and on, in such vibrance. Wet light
gave the leaves' undersides a tinfoil glint.
Rag and bone bushland. White arms lifted, dangling
cloth. That chant. What it was all about I forgot.

A Winter Morning

For a few more minutes now, all the day's furniture
will remain sheeted in a shuttered room.
With their glow of sucked-thin barely sugar
the lights way off at the by-pass still drooping in bloom.
Here, there are only two headlights, on a lane,
easing downstairs. In wood and fibro, my cathedral town—
such this valley. *Materia* is *mater*; substance is womb.

I go along backyard fences through some fog—
most of these are patched with old corrugated iron—
onto a plumed, translating hillslope, with someone's dog;

high up, the sky is lifting, become woodgrain:
its whirls, dabs, darts, long streaks of golden cloud,
on airiest blue. The weeds' strung fruits wear a globed
insect's opal glitter. I skirt the dank tree-line . . .

Those eucalyptus are the blue of husky voices.
Their elevations, declivities have all of them accents
flying. I'm here on a Sunday alone, for the offices
of matter—poinsettias, more red than sacraments;
a sceptred palm-tree's golden smoulder; this insouciance
of levitated pink; grass's lime effulgence . . .
It is the same lesson: ease of their relinquishments.

The Lake

open
screendoor

seashells

wireless
murmur

bathroom
water

louvres

ballooning
light

After Writing All Day

A deep blueness of water—the deep blue water
of an afternoon, when light's being trumpeted long-
    stemmed
from among buildings, and above the harbour;
when the light is an ornament, not yet crepuscular,
a baroque, passing into rococo goldenness; then,
with the clouds like pale acid stains, purple-hemmed,
or a few lupin-fringed bales on limitless tundra,
this blue is the windfall of withered heaven.

Slowly as a leaky tap, the moored yachts melt. Globule
loosened after spreading globule; each slips
thickly away, wobbling, dissolving. And beneath the
    Council
trees, I lean on a balustrade. The harbour's pestle
works salt. Underlit, a tree's nude arms, water-
moulded, undulate; the leaves crowd with polyps'
density, though flat. Opposite, bushland—that bauble;
cramped, introvert. We look to each other.

It is towed by the city: freakish, subsidized, marginal.
Sometimes, when here, I'm dissatisfied to be a poet—
too isolate, like being a deacon or homosexual.
Yet I've loved such writing, "direct, sensuous, musical",
above all I might do; since that's to savour one's
own life, and to add savour. Over there, the intricate,
lit bush will be simmering with scent; and the paths tunnel
amid such vivid surging, such freehand lines.

There are things not for everyone, and perhaps it's better:
look at things that are. Those most appreciative
make an *aristos*. (If genuine.) Plumed at cheeks and each
    finger,

chilly, I turn home. And the sleeping bag, I remember,
thinking of blueness. It is soft and full as a blouse,
in the back yard. From time in the weather, so alive
it's germinating pale fern-shoots all over,
almost too light and large-souled to get into the house.

Small Town

Lime-green, all the lowbeamed
headlights coming by on
smoky orange dusk;
in holiday file they cross
white neon of a service station.

Much later, she again looks out,
when the highway is
a smear of grease,
and the Milky Way's blowing there,
a feather in space.

Mist

The tall trees are making a dark ravine
about this long reach of the creek
that is dark and heavy as a marble slab.
It's just before daybreak.

On the water's surface, as though teased
or kinked, there stand

fibrils of mist, balancing. Underwater,
that way, a spineless plant

lies upward. These mist-weeds
are the little splashes made by shredding
cotton wool, for a diorama.
Their suspension's really a wallowing

in slowness. It occurs on the paddocks,
too, where a single rag
is reared, eerily as the horse-head
nebula, over the other fog.

—Something mesmerized, sipped by the air.
Clumpy or steepled as African huts,
tree-shapes are awash in a milky smoke
that's part of witch-doctors' rites.

Fog lingers, like white pullet feathers,
or fibres of feathers, on a woman's
busily-plucking hands. Hands ruddy and white
and thick-wristed.—The sun's

going to baste and make succulent
this earth. Even though fed with gags,
the truth will speak—will dissolve them.
Even if dead, a wet sheet that is sagged

across the empty hole of its mouth
will steam, will flutter. Or the hero's skin,
red and flawless, shall come forth
to accuse, as the bandages are undone.

History's a story of loss and betrayal,
and yet we're led by the earth to persevere.
Light analyses the lubricants in dew.
Only sawmill haze left in the air.

A Summer Evening

They still do as was always done:
they call the children just one night
then make sure of the fly-screen catch,
while moths knock down a shaggy pinch
off themselves or the porch light.

And insects race their bobbins, thick
as a sweat shop, as grass itch,
as matted grass seeds that are stuck
smudgily in bleached leg-hairs.
Another sound: a nutmeg-grater scratch.

It is the time to "Look at yourselves!"
One who's not a parent gazes out
at tree-shapes spread like peacocks on
a lake, the town; at grass-loop shine;
at the empty lit set-up of this street.

And likes the way the paling fence below
is reclining into weeds. A thickened tree
by the house has its bole brush-swiped
with shadow. At this time a milkman came.
Now, the marching-girl movements of t.v.

A horse crops close around arc-lights'
twin metal poles, in the paddock next door,
that rise from concrete for a car-yard
and make a light of grainy plastic there;
the horse, snapped from a speeding car.

Another way, the neon badges, and trees
rank as weeds; that last squeezed light,
beautiful and calm—as when illness emptied
her face. And you had thought, Why not
like this always? Why too late?

Nine Bowls of Water

Clear water, in silvery tin dishes
dented as ping pong balls:
a lemon juice tinge of the staling light is in them;
they've a faint lid of dust.

A potted water along a board slopped
and dripping lightly.
While the men work on the city road, excavating
its charred blackness,

the water waits
behind a corrugated tin shed that is set
at the pavement front,
under a tall shadowing empty stadium.

On the low plank, also, crude soap pieces,
bright as the fat
of gutted chickens—but, with a closer look, resistant,
darkly-cracked, like old bone handles.

One beside each bowl,
and the rags are on their bits of hooked wire.
The cars continue,
but few people walk here between the lunch shed

and brick wall. Set out along a wet bench,
the kneeling water:
this reality from which we have dreamed the spirit.
We walk in grittiness,

on papers, mud-scrapings,
splattered with a sporadic jackhammer racket,
past nine bowls of water—a gallantry of the union.
Trees in avenues and sailing boats and women.

Under the Summer Leaves

1

Every morning we left the wooden hotel
and crossed the estuary along a footbridge,
that had some of its planks and lengths of rail missing,
going to the sandhills and the surfing beach.
The bridge made a tilting, crooked line
into the tops of a mangrove swamp,
the round leaves of which were shinily green
as small tree frogs. Stepping off the long boardwalk
on the far shore, close to the river's flexed arm,
we found the water deepened after the bend,
blocked from the mangroves with a low breakwater,
and here it became a peacock's purplish-blue,
always fluttering in the seabreeze.
The jumbled stone breakwater running ahead of us dragged
a taut rein at the river's bending neck.
We walked on a track between that granite,
of waist-height, and the swamp trees
from out of black sand—those insect legs and torsos
of pandanus, and the mangroves, overlapping
so densely, they immediately obscured their reserve.
Small crabs were sprayed from our shadows backwards,
glaring stalk-eyed and showing open claws—
each was like a cricketer who reverse-pedals,
demanding "Mine!" We'd look behind,
over the river's broad, slewed cornering,
and see the blue hotel—steep-roofed
as though the gaudy, watched-over descendant
of the gentian-coloured hills. Beside the hotel
was a fused mass of pines,
and this seemed to have drawn from out of those mornings
all of their sediment, all their darkness.

Then going on, into the heath, towards the green
vine-covered sandhills, on which slant

white paths were slashed—winding adrift, in high grass,
for the two hundred yards of a natural category.
A matt green and russet country, seemingly so drab,
that's of a texture more rich than all
the agricultural shows' embroidery stands.
The whitest sand, or salted grey sandstone, underfoot.
A few eucalyptus, wind-crook'd
and loosely splattered with leaves, are there,
flesh-white, smooth, unyielding; isolate
above a close detail from an Old Master—a smoky dark
and the drips of rose madder and yellow ochre;
above those brushes, with their scumblings;
over the broomhead coarseness, the fur,
spines, horse-combs, pennants, and fine white flowers
that float, wind-borne, like splintered water.

For transcendence, we've the clouds of autumn,
the clouds of summer, that build plinth on plateau,
and then vast cupolas, and billow
as though Renaissance draperies; modelled with a wash
and Tiepolo soft. One comes upon these best
across the dry heath country of the Coast.

But first, each day, we'd have to pass
a last great complicated trunkless mangrove,
sprouting myriad-limbed off the earth,
and every time, a man would be standing in there,
amid its crooked mesh of shadows.
He remained very still, his back to the path
on which a few people walked—
the young boardriders, reluctantly returning,
lugging a short board against the hip,
their broad faces with a white stripe, sullen and stolid
like dripping steers; the shrill girls
keeping to their own groups, brown as a baker's shop, and
        carrying
radios long as suitcases, wispy salt afloat

above their shoulders, and on the foreshores of their chests;
and sometimes older people, going outwards,
unemployed fishermen, pensioners, wearing floral hats
and towels like astrakhan collars,
in their seaweed idleness.
That man was leaned slightly against a thick branch,
one hand propped along it, never glancing
as we came by. Although he was shaded with a lattice,
you could see he was an Aboriginal
by the hand from a sleeve, and the igneous bones
of the last quarter of his face.
There were bottles everywhere about his feet
but never any foodscraps or paper, nor signs of a camp.
An aurora of immense, pure, colourless light
would be vaulting upwards ahead of us
within an absolute shade of blueness; vaulting on itself
and upon itself
like the felt streamings of a gas flame,
from beyond the sandhills, and their grandstand view.

When I was growing up around there, that place had been
just another small town off the highway,
with mothy streetlights, a motel's insomnia,
treeroots under the pavement blocks,
broken fences and long yards, white fibro
beyond the trees' broad shadows,
bougainvilleas, weatherboards.
Now there were split-level Spanish houses
in an estate across the hillslopes. There was the first
tall block of flats. Tourists were driving
to the beach, along a new road; and out there, you found,
was also getting freckled over.
Now the cars and motorbikes were everywhere,
their tyre-marks drawn about the sand
like great tangled ropes—so that people might seem
a lynch mob, threatening everything that's natural.
Technology both gives and removes us from the world—
hardly ever increases our ability to experience it;

rather, speed and ease mean uninvolvement,
and so condescension, remoteness, emptiness.

Each morning we'd stay in the surf for hours,
then lie at a slant among the sandhills
to watch the bumping approach of the ocean;
to hear the waves pile-driven,
and see the boardriders slip backwards from them.
We saw how as the waves advanced, they'd disperse,
transversely, a running whiteness,
as though shed by a plough-share;
the whole rostered ocean, lifted upon its lifting,
would stall blue-green a second, and then fire
a white flare, to meet a similar trajectory
from further along its folding water,
before all was lost, on their collision,
in the complete collapse of the house;
in a white chaos,
as when a snow-laden pine tree is felled into deep snow.

That town, beyond the river bank, was now
a main street of new brick shops, all
a contused dull red, and shaped like public lavatories,
but with advertising over the windows,
on the flat rooftops, above the pavement;
a place of thongs, and of shorts tilted under stomachs;
of loud cars making fast getaways,
then returning in a few minutes;
of poker machines, video porn, real estate agents,
and pop music wallowing from the wide-open supermarket,
with its leering or lachrymose imagery, as in
a fairground mirror; of the tarry electric wires
slung low across everything.
In the rowdy bars were the appetites
like a steel rod draped in flesh. We could see,
from the hotel's empty first floor verandah,
from the one old building that remained,
how people had come there out of the cities
and had built the packed suburb of the caravan park.

Some day there'll be nothing but urban men—
I imagined their lives as like that shuffling water,
tepid, brackish, and shallow,
over the sandbank in the silted river.

We used to go again to the sea of an evening;
the only ones to tire, it seemed,
of the pounding and clamour at the pub,
that was like the tugging of a bonfire,
in which you could feel their rage for more.
We'd find a cool breeze out there
after the narcotic afternoon,
and moonlight strewn on the green-black ocean
looked like a scattering of shaved ice.
We wondered if the Aboriginal was sleeping then
under his tree, or drinking alone,
but it was too dark to say, and we'd no wish
to interfere. We often spoke of him, casuistically,
"as the breeze sighs through the withered fern".
All we guessed was he must be a half-caste,
coming from there. Of a day, for nearly a week,
every time we went out to the ocean, and again no matter
how long we stayed, he'd be standing
in the wide tree that flung its branches
immediately off the sand. He occasionally took a sip,
and always looked in one direction, his hand lightly
on a bough—gazing over the suede,
buff-coloured reeds, above the low swamp trees,
and through a faint salt-dust in the air, towards,
or so it seemed (although probably he couldn't have seen
a thing), but if you followed his gaze,
towards a particular mountain, blue
and symmetrical, and stuccoed faintly
along its edges with a forest line; one that was stepping
forward, fluted, out of the range, and
that lifted to its node of satisfaction.
A mountain piled there as though it were something
trickled up on the pan of a scale.

2

This town we'd thought our holiday from the future.
We had come there after months in Japan—
back out of the tunnel Australia was entering.
From Tokyo, Osaka, Nagoya,
Kyoto and Hiroshima: those places of a constant smoke,
like bushfire days, of chemical stench, unending concrete;
cities run together, and superimposing on each other;
that people made seem, each, a shattered ants' nest.
In Japan, they have named the steep, unusable mountains
national parks (that are the calendar face
of their country), but had found a new use for them:
during our stay, a campaign had begun for blasting these,
so as to add to their territory sideways.
The Japanese could do this.
Already they bulldoze the hills for lime,
to kerb and gutter the coast; and rivers are straightened
and lined with concrete, the word for which translates
"correcting" the river. And yet, they sentimentalize
on nature. Plastic autumn leaves are hung out
from the light posts, in Tokyo's treeless streets.
The Japanese attitude really is,
"If its back points to the heavens, then eat it."
Lift a plating off the live lobster's back
and take with chopsticks that wet porridge
while its fronds
counterpoint the controlled pick.
Nature is just an approved view.
At prescribed places on the Hokkaido highway
one has a prescribed response.
Though, now you must censor for yourself
the pylons, in swathes, all akimbo like armoured samurai,
the chimneys, or reactors, that jostle a relic—
those moss-padded rocks, the bamboos parted
on a temple, that is hollow as a movie set. You will find
the camera's a fine pair of blinkers.

Nature manipulated, miniaturized is the preference
where earth and weather are so treacherous.
No one really cares there to live in the country:
a people of such centripetal impulse
they pack into cities, that are always
square-limbed and brutal as their printed *kanji*—
where nature's only the moon
(and not the air, certainly), fallen into a dust-grey sky
in summer, like a big rotting persimmon, or
in winter, on a dusk that is mauve and furry as a crystal,
a salt-white precipitate, at the bottom of a tube—
they pack into cities, and into those trains
that, if spruce, are only cattle trucks, and
as in their houses, keep all the windows closed in summer.

You begin to imagine things that might be done
by a country where so many
are still at their desks, when you pass on a lifting train
the ice-cube trays of office lights
toward midnight, and you learn
there they remain
until the overseer has decided to go home.

The Bomb's of more influence in Japan than the Buddha:
they have suffered power, and will now assert it.
(Though, the major tradition has long been the Confucianist,
with its utterly entangling obligations,
its narrowness of sympathy, its servilities.)
Buddhism is dead, like an empty crab shell—
except, there is something of the name which is an
        inversion,
invented by a kind of Norman Vincent Peale.
A professor said to me, The things you admire
of the past (Ryokan's poems, restraint, rock gardens)
only belonged to an elite: it was they
who listened to bamboos, and the eaves dripping,

who viewed the moon, and wrote
poems for each other; they who could wander
from temple to temple, or stay in some grass hut
on their own. Ordinary people, in those times,
weren't allowed even a family name—they worked, they got
    drunk,
they'd the bath house, and the raucous theatre;
for them, the forest was closed and dim;
if you weren't a diver then
(until Meiji, in 1860, or even until MacArthur),
you had no business to swim.
Released by the capitalists, by their mode of production,
this class lacks a taste for the Japanese past.
They prefer *kitsch*. And their possessing it
so vastly—from Big Macs and Coca Cola
to plastic woodgrain and fluffiness to Mickey Mouse—
is all we can mean, when we say they are rich.

So my arriving there was a goodbye. And yet, for what
they contribute to Utopia, gratitude.
It was myself I found, in their imagery.
Those polished long floorboards, which are of a day
moonlit. The forest where a berry fell
onto a pool, and a white bird flew
in the dark halls. The bamboo flute, lifting to wander
as a crane's wings. And Zen masters like Dōgen, who when
    he dipped
water from a stream, in the bamboo dipper,
poured half back, before he would drink, since
he felt all things as interdependent.
Now there are others, who believe themselves humbled
in their own faces, and before the lank-voiced Americans,
before all "red-faced and merely physical
Westerners", and these grasp at things,
but without lumber room, and so they have potential
like turbine waters, stashed downwards
in darkening strata,

and growing heavier. And yet, they also must see
how just outside that always low-burning, respectful light
all the qualities beyond mechanism
have blown away, fast
as smoke-shapes over grass.
Their lives are in all human ways
much worse than these in the loose-end-of-town cities
of the world, the Australian cities. Free trade,
no doubt, will sell us to their obsessions:
to that religion, the one Japanese family; to the demands
of a mask, cruel as lacquer.

Although the purpose of travel is homesickness
I achieved it too soon in Tokyo—
a city where only warehouses face the water.
When I saw this I knew,
for all my love of things in their culture,
and though I'd received there much formularized kindness,
it is with *Die Natur*
that my loyalties are.

One late night in Tokyo, when I was walking
near where I stayed, in a working-class district,
I felt the back-lane streets
all around me, stickily as a web, and saw them, as if from
    above,
tight like the crazing on a glaze.
The tram wires were tangled great molasses strings,
hung in a fast, low steam. The few small trucks
and quiet cyclists flowed quickly
into those dark capillaries. And then, for minutes,
a bubble stillness. No one seemed about, and yet I knew
there were people everywhere,
close by, behind the old wood and oil paper. I went on
more deeply, and came up to the fine, cold smirk
on the face of a fox god, above oranges
and incense sticks, in a shrine at a dim corner.
The dishcloth sky was wrung of its few stale drops.

I was in a dense forest: wall to wall houses,
each of them three paces wide, adobe-shaped, of concrete,
deal planks and bamboo. Above all that,
on the low purple clouds, so lurid and cinematic,
there was more, blocks of flats,
all thirty stories, and slung of a day with futons and
      washing,
but that night only some lights,
like computers left on, in their obscure rank on rank.
And shadows of smoke hove across these;
smoke still rolling out of the factories—in the cold air
becoming as dense and deeply-gathered
as the wool of a ram's neck; and this was being added
to the bales always piling there.
Then I came to a closed market street: a place
I had seen with its stalls open,
amid the bicycles' chrome occlusions. A usual
Asian market, all steam and broken-toothed screeching,
the forearms complicit in skewerings,
those barrels of flensed squid, protoplasmic,
and vegetables sinking through the spectrum of rot.
That night in the silent, flushed-out street
the closed fish stall was rank
like a raw, coarse smell of ocean—
so that I saw at once a long jetty, out of my boyhood's
foolishness. One I used to clamber underneath,
self-testing, of a night; coming back
along its charcoal-black, slippery
calligraphy, until the night I fell,
had fallen, into the ragged, freezing salt-solution
that burned at my skin
and the filigree membranes inside my head. And there,
baptised in shock, I'd felt myself kidnapped
one-handedly, transferred
on a big swell,
off into the emigrant harbour; dangling
my legs in a steel lift-well. I saw
across a smoky beach, and empty dunes, the streetlights,

weakly blue, and the top floors of the hotel,
bulged with light; and heard,
as with a faulty memory, bits of what
the dance band played. I knew myself alone
with a sea-diluted voice;
where I seemed to have forgotten
how, even, to get out of my jacket. And I'd a sort of vision
    there,
for a moment, of the dining room table at home
as my plate was being removed.

And then I was remembering Japan,
above the bright estuary, in a hotel room.
Gauze curtains were blowing in the wardrobe mirror,
there was sand on the lino, swim trunks
hung from the door, and the loose holiday crowd
was outside, the thong-flapping Australians,
flickering or yelling, through the enormous light.
And I saw we are much as the Japanese are—
all "determined by the means of production";
the same machines, or machine-profferments,
allure us, and have shaped us all.
We're all sentimentalists of a Millennium,
who cannot conceive there is wealth in not having.

Every afternoon of the holiday it would rain—
how it comes down
on that part of the Coast, for about an hour,
from almost exactly 3.00, in the summer.
Under a dense, potato-shaped cloud,
with its black loam, its nightshade tinge of green,
a hair-root is suddenly struck.
And in the west, along a compressed zone
of aniseed tint, an urgently-running cardiogram.
The light dims for a matinee,
and clouds are dilated in the shape of bellowing;
then rain flies like a silvery train;
and there are long rumblings, as though a bridge upheld it.

All the country grows loose in the rain.
I had a front seat, out by the railing,
and onto that gloom would leap
the wonderful high look
of the wings of Samothrace, whenever the banana trees
    were lit.
It would end too soon,
with long drips as in a water tank;
with a creaking and shuffle on the tin roof
lightly, like Fred Astaire.

Once, after the rain, I walked from town,
by the seedpod fences, along the rammed earth of a road
on which double tyre-marks shone
far into the cellular afternoon. And the road shone again
in ellipses toward the hills.
The sun had come back, carrying its skirts
among the trees; and so I turned
in there, onto a track. Every leaf poised its medicine drops.
The ivory paddocks gleamed
beyond fire-blackened stringybarks
that had the texture and sheen of crushed velvet.
The lily pads shone
on a swamp of tobacco brown—
those shapes out of which the frogs are inflated.
A long-fronded, elated afternoon.
There was a rhythm among the saplings from Tom Roberts,
and paperbarks that Nolan has taught us to see.
I came out on a hillslope above the lilac ocean.
Light on the clouds opposite sunset
was like that in the foyer of a seashell.
White eucalyptus rose about me in front of the sea, their
    leaves
long like green parakeets.
The mind easily fragments within such dimensions: I felt it
    poise
far above, a second, as I was leaning
there, on the moist, thin rind

which is all that is delicacy, all that's edible fruit,
of this country. Then I realized how probably the land
I had just walked over was already owned
in some boardroom of Hong Kong or Japan. And all I'd just
    seen
became things that lay in a fire
in the moment when they still have their form.